Once for the Last Bandit

Other books by Samuel Hazo

Poetry
  Discovery
  The Quiet Wars
  Listen with the Eye (with photographs by James P. Blair)
  My Sons in God
  Blood Rights
  Twelve Poems (with intaglios by George Nama)

Translation
  The Blood of Adonis

Criticism
  Hart Crane: An Introduction and Interpretation

Fiction
  Seascript: A Mediterranean Logbook

Anthology
  A Selection of Contemporary Religious Poetry

Once for the Last Bandit

NEW AND
PREVIOUS POEMS
BY
SAMUEL
HAZO

University
of Pittsburgh
Press

Library of Congress Catalog Card Number 74–181397
ISBN 0–8229–3240–7
Copyright © 1972, Samuel Hazo
All rights reserved
Henry M. Snyder & Co., Inc., London
Manufactured in the United States of America

Acknowledgment is made to the following journals and magazines in which some of the poems in this collection first appeared: *The American Scholar, Approach, The Antioch Review, The Atlantic, The Barat Review. The Beloit Poetry Journal, The Bennington Review, The Borestone Mountain Awards 1960, The Carolina Quarterly, Chicago Choice, Commonweal, The Critic, Fine Arts Calendar, Harper's, The Kenyon Review, Ktaadn, Jubilee, Lotus, The Malahat Review, The Mediterranean Review, The Mill Mountain Review, The Minnesota Review, Mundus Artium, The New Orleans Review, New World Writing, The New York Times, The North American Review, Pennsylvania Culture, Perspective, Poetry Bag, Poetry Northwest, Prairie Schooner, The Saturday Review, The Sewanee Review, The Transatlantic Review, The University of Kansas City Review, Varlik, The Virginia Quarterly Review, Voyages,* and *The Yale Review.*

Discovery and Other Poems and *The Quiet Wars* were first published by Sheed and Ward, Inc. (copyright © 1959, 1962).

To my wife, Anne,
and our son, Samuel Robert

Contents

Contents (continued)

Contents (continued)

Contents (continued)

A NOTE TO THE UNDERSTANDERS

Sorting through poems from your previously published books is like looking at old photographs of yourself. They are all undeniably you; they are the way you looked then. But there are inevitably some that seem more *you* than others. So it is with poems. You deny none, but, if you are compelled to choose, there are some you affirm more than others. Perhaps a certain style links them. Perhaps they touch themes that were then and still seem to you the only ones worth the ink. This collection then contains my affirmations from *Discovery, The Quiet Wars, Listen with the Eye, My Sons in God,* and *Blood Rights.* It concludes with *Once for the Last Bandit,* which can be read as a single poem or as many poems but which, in any case, is when and where I am. But not why. Poetry can answer many questions, but not that one.

SAMUEL HAZO

Discovery

DIMINUENDO

It was a time of diminution,
little Fay.
I watched you scatter jacks
across a hopscotched road—
a time for play.

In me you saw the stranger
children see.
You picked, picked up jacks,
then silenced both your hands
between your knees.

FOR A SON WHO WILL NEVER BE BORN

When poplars spire stripped and brittle sticks
toward December stars, you will not see
the first ice catch and thicken at the curbs.
Balked of their first and last parenthesis,
the years will leave you winterless and free.

You will not know the exile's day, the nights
of thunder when the night is thunderless
and cloudless as the dark before your eyes,
nor will you grudge the waves of westering light
and the blood-bright sun ascending wonderless . . .

Less brave than Simeon, I speak my fear
for flesh not yet created, named or known . . .
He blessed a child begotten crucified
and mocked with a prophecy all I would spare
you with these fostering, futile words, my son.

PARACHUTIST

After jump, drop and somersault
with cords unraveling in skein,
chute rising in a puff more taut
than sail until it domes a cone
of cords hooked to a harnessed dot
twirling and suspended like a toy
wind-swung and puppeted in space,
he pendulums sideways down the sky.

LULL

Owls swoop low over flagless poles.
Battalions bivouacked on a maneuver
sleep platooned in a Quonset town.

Dungarees rinse dry under the moon,
billowing with a suavity of banners
as buglers barrack the last patrols.

The Quiet Wars

POSTSCRIPT TO MANY LETTERS

For Robert George Hazo

While other brothers meet and talk like foes
or strangers or alumni—hostile, cool
or banal—, brotherhood is still our binding.
Somehow we have survived disintegration
since the quiet, Pittsburgh afternoons we walked
in rain bareheaded, scarfless, flaunting health,
the nights we smoked large, academic pipes
and read and talked philosophy, the years
of seminars and uniforms and trips
and letters postmarked Paris, Quantico,
Beirut, Jerusalem and San Francisco.

Nothing has changed or failed and still we have
"the same heroes and think the same men fools."
Our heroes still are individuals
resolved to face their private absolutes.
We see the fool in all who fail themselves
by choice and turn all promise cold with talk.
A Levantine who saw such folly done
two thousand years ago grew bored with life
and said only the unborn were worth blessing.
Not sticks, not any, not the sharpest stones
can bruise or break the unbegotten bones.

Yet, fools and our few heroes will persist.
We cannot bless the unborn flesh nor wish
our times and cities back to countrysides
when wigwams coned into a twist of poles.
The future holds less answers than the past.

Salvation lies in choice, in attitude,
in faith that mocks glib gospelers who leave
the name of Jesus whitewashed on a cliff.
We still can shun what shames or shams the day
and keep as one our vigor in the bond
of blood where love is fierce but always fond.

TO MY MOTHER

Had you survived that August afternoon
of sedatives, you would be sixty-three,
and I would not be rummaging for words
to plot or rhyme what I would speak to you.

Tonight I found a diary you kept
in 1928, and while I read
your script in English, Arabic and Greek,
I grudged those perished years and nearly wept

and cursed whatever god I often curse
because I scarcely knew one day with you
or heard you sing or call me by my name.
I know you were a teacher and a nurse

and sang at all the summer festivals.
You made one scratched recording of a song
I often play when no one else is home,
but that is all I have to keep you real.

The rest exists in fragile photographs,
a sudden memoir in my father's eyes
and all the anecdotes of thirty years
remembered like a portrait torn in half

and torn in half again until a word
deciphered in a diary rejoins
these tatters in my mind to form your face
as magically as music overheard

can summon and assemble everything
about a day we thought forever past.
For one recovered second you are near.
I almost hear you call to me and sing

before the world recoils and returns . . .
I have no monument, my beautiful,
to offer you except these patterned lines.
They cannot sound the silentness that burns

and burns although I try to say at last
there lives beyond this treachery of words
your life in me anew and in that peace
where nothing is to come and nothing past.

FOR MY GRANDFATHER

Someone should speak a word for you
who after all lived only long
enough to teach us children's songs
in Arabic remembered now

with times you strung your lute alone
and plucked it with an eagle's plume
while we sat quiet, small and calm
and heard you sing of Lebanon

until our days of roundelays
turned brief as breathing, and the vengeance
of cathedrals tolled to silence
all your love and all your minstrelsy.

PROGENITOR

A stern, mustachioed Assyrian
who stalked the animals that Adam named
and searched the desert where the chariots
and all the legions of Sennacherib
advanced their blazonry toward the sea,
my father's father hunted porcupines
a rifleshot from Nineveh and Eden.

I know him only from my father's tales,
this Aramaic sire who brought his sons
beyond the havoc of the scimitar
by mule from Mosul to Jerusalem
and somehow I lived a century and ten
before he died and left his youngest son
this son to hymn his bones in Babylon.

THE PAPER ECHO

Barnum's trapeze above the horseback girl
beheads two boxers juxtaposed in trunks
with white and negro knuckles taped in gloves
and cocked for now forgotten uppercuts.

Before electorates of sidewalk kids
a sheriff grins for last November's votes.
Mustached with mud, a blonde forever dives
from sherbet mountains into lakes of beer.

This bleaching billboard's hieroglyphist ,
I solve its wintered puzzles strip by strip.
From circus heavyweights to swimmer's toes
I let what clues these peelings chronicle

cipher blear fragments of a garbled film
reeled crazy but eternal in my brain
while posters tattered in the sun betray
shadows of Plato's den, and so the world.

PREFACE TO
A POETRY READING

Since eyes are deaf and ears are blind to words
in all their ways, I speak the sounds I write,
hoping you see what somehow stays unheard
and hear what never is quite clear at sight.

CHALLENGE

Leveling his pole like some quixotic lance,
trotting, trotting faster, faster to his mark,
slotting the pole, twisting upward to a bar,
contortioning clear, the vaulter drops in sand.

He wipes his hands and stumbles from the pit
with sand still sweated to his thighs and calves,
retrieves the pole and drags it like a mast
behind him down the cinder aisle, and waits.

I feel in my onlooker's hands the taped
and heavy barrel of the vaulter's pole
and see the bar notched higher for his leap.
His spikes clench earth, and all my muscles pull
to face a task with nothing but my skill
and struggle for the mark I must excel.

TRANSITION

A collar weighted with lieutenant's bars
made his a face to be saluted once
and possibly despised by one platoon
I marched ten miles in Norfolk fahrenheit.
Close-order-drill made me the martinet
I tried to tame, but Adam in my blood
inclined to epaulets until each stance
and striding flexed my sinews for command.

Soft holsters felt familiar at my hip,
and bayonets drove easily through groins
of dummies gallowed for the practice thrusts
like snakes impaled and twisting on a tine
to ready me for months of counting cash.
Released, I paid myself my vouchered sum
with bills that curved my wallet like a stave
and drove the pre-paid mileage into days

of typing theses in quintuplicate
and teaching boys the Latin ablative.
Surrendering by barracked ways meant more
than wearing out my military socks.
I kept a wry reservist's look for half
a year and still keep step with walkers-by
although I hate the spectacle of squads
paced to a cadence in a drummed parade.

Between the sweep and sudden cease of grace
I wage today the quiet wars of art
with students calmly primed to probe my views
in lectures I cannot pre-think or plan.
I tell them only what I right now know.
I ask them only what they right now see
and take some triumph from each day's defeat
in mine and everybody's war and peace.

HER SON, MY STUDENT

I came averse to wakes with nothing apt
or soothing to arrange the anteroom
that burst with sobs, bouquets and bannered wreaths.
Before the mother I could only say
I taught the boy in school for half a year.
I walked away defeated by her tears

and walked all evening lost within her loss.
Wild sumacs bent beneath the falling walls
of wind, and clouds developed in the dark
like ice on zero lakes or frost on glass.
I hoped someone would come and call my name,
but no one knew me there, and no one came.

CAROL OF A BRIDE

When sacred subterfuge of blood subsides
and we lie near but neuter in the dark,
may I be like the body of a bird
suspended by the hushed and gliding wings
of this surrender, buoyant in a flight
of yielding that redeems and will not leave
me naked as Eve deserted in Eden.

I pray for sons to bootprint fields of snow
and trudge together up the runnered slopes
before they shout and fling themselves on sleds
to race beyond the winters of my fear.
Let them hurrah the sun with summering
or hide in grass and smoke catalpa pods
like peaceful Choctaws puffing calumets.

May I be loved but spared surviving you.
Survival is not life but living on
between the noon and midnight of a loss
where no one shall await the equinox
nor calm my cries if I should wake from dreams
and say your name to nothing but the night,
and say your name to nothing but the night.

CAROL OF A FATHER

He runs ahead to ford a flood of leaves—
he suddenly a forager and I
the lagging child content to stay behind
and watch the gold upheavals at the curb
submerge his surging ankles and subside.

A word could leash him back or make him turn
and ask me with his eyes if he should stop.
One word, and he would be a son again
and I a father sentenced to correct
a boy's caprice to shuffle in the drifts.

Ignoring fatherhood, I look away
and let him roam in his Octobering
to mint the memories of those few falls
when a boy can wade the quiet avenues
alone, and the sound of leaves solves everything.

THE CARNIVAL ARK

Their bodies hourglassed and multiplied
by mirrors warped beside the handrail route
and angled to reflect reflected faces
to infinity, the crowds invade the ark
that rolls obedient to hidden engines
Noah never knew when he survived
the forty days and forty nights of rain.

Mounted in the tipping fo'c's'le, Noah's wife
stares dumbly at the slowing Ferris wheel,
the roller coasters rocketing and clacking
down the tunneled rails, the clowns with blown
balloons aloft and moored like zeppelins
to carts where popcorn bounces into bloom
and ping-pongs lightly on the buttered glass.

Quick jets of air spurt upward from the deck,
and skirts umbrella out like capes to show
the gartered hose or vaccinated thighs
to gawkers-by, but Noah never breaks
his vigil for the peaks of Ararat
now just beginning to emerge between
the spookhouse and the Coca-Cola lights.

BETWEEN YOU AND ME

A girl in yellow slacks kept watching me
as I slapped down a dime and palmed the three
lopsided baseballs just before I threw
and three times missed the pyramided pints.
I changed a dollar into dimes and threw
and missed again, but still the girl looked on
like someone waiting to applaud or boo.
Try throwing with a strange girl watching you.

Black-breasted Balinese, a bowl of gourds,
enormous trays for ashes, checker boards
and dolls attired as duchesses or nuns
sparkled like booty on the winner's shelf.
I threw and threw until my shirtback clung
adhesively and cold against my spine.
It was no more a case of having fun.
I swore I would keep throwing till I won.

I tried with all my will to concentrate
and pitched the final baseball hard and straight
at three damn target pints still left in line.
They broke like bottles shattered by a shot.
I turned to see if Yellow Slacks had seen,
but she was gone, and with her went my need
to win a wreath or some cheap figurine
to show the world, if you know what I mean.

MARIE WITH THE TATTOOED BELLY

"Shatter the oyster and pluck the pearl
that mounts the ring that wears the girl,"
whispers Marie with the tattooed belly,
dancing in spangles and sauntering slyly
in front of applauders who find it funny
to see her shimmy the snake on her tummy.

"Shatter the mirror that shows the years,
bind me with blindfolds, smother my ears,"
whimpers Marie with the tattooed belly,
tired of trancing and wandering slowly
away from applauders who throw her money
and find quite funny the snake on her tummy.

GETTYSBURG

In iron where their horses reared and neighed,
the mounted generals survey like scouts
long rows of rusting cannon wheeled abreast
and aimed at Appalachian fields scarecrowed
with sculptured infantry in statuesque
attack before the ridge of Pickett's rout.

Necklaced with Kodaks and binoculars,
June tourists range beyond the battlements
to search for richochets in trunks of trees
or photograph old barns with shrapnel scars,
the pledge of Lincoln on a plaque of brass
and graves that hold the bones of regiments.

Cold iron and the quarried stone rehearse
past carnage in a frieze of history.
Hard replicas replace the buried boys
who shook no fists against the universe.
They charged the barricades and were destroyed
where tourists grimly talk photography.

THE ARMISTICE PARADE

See guidons lift the speared and twisting fish
of pennons to the winds; hear drummers lash
drums swung in unison while tubas blare
blunt sputters puffed through convoluted brass.

Lieutenants dress their columns, hold salutes
and volley long commands to launch brigades
beneath confetti sleet and flags that twitch
sporadically as horsetails from their staves.

Reserved for wars we number now to keep
the first and second straight for history,
this new breed struts before the kiddee crowds
to blur with noise those Argonne jamborees

when riflefire drummed old ranks to dig
and snail themselves like embryos in sties
until Foch told the brass to call it off
and Wilson faced the music at Versailles.

A rooster flexing a wing at a time, testing
each leg for a step, a calf's saliva smeared
and frozen to its pelt, the stanchioned cow
with wrinkled udders cold until they swell
and soften in my milking palms and cross
their steaming bursts in buckets vised by knees,
a bull obliviously munching mash
or fodder in a sideways chomp of jaws,
the barn cathedral-still, alfalfa baled
with cloverhay and storied to the beams,
an uncooped chicken pecking at the planks . . .

of barrack bunks, sleepers clippered to the scalp,
shared mirrors for shaves, the squat of soldiers grim
and sallow-flanked in defecation, webs
of fungus in a riflethong removed
before inspection, manual-of-arms,
exchanged salutes, the upright duffel bags
unpacked in heated huts in Quantico,
chiggers in neckflesh and underneath the belt,
disburser's fingers gritty with the dirt
of money, generals reviewing right-
faced ranks, a daub of cosmoline on butts . . .

of slim cigars, a saunter down the dark
of streets where squad cars idle at a curb
like hounds alert to follow shortwaved spoors,
of war bonds cashed to pay a spindled stack
of bills at each semester's summoning,
placement directors flanked by telephones,

a quiver of sharpened pencils splayed point up
from drinking cups beside their doodler's pads,
the gravestone of a nameplate on a desk,
the antiseptic cleanliness of schools
at dawn, freshmen confused by Caesar's wars . . .

through poetry with English majors tense
in dialectic, furious with truth,
the way of kisses, rings and marrying,
waking to a wife, contour of womanshape
beneath a quilt, the fingers loose with sleep,
the fierce ballet of baseball in July,
the Adirondack noons when matted boards
buck upward with a snap to catapult
the divers flexed into the roped-off deep,
two uncles buried, one in rain and one
in torpor, nephews againg as I age.

Buried in my blood the farm, the dust of hay,
the foxholes spaded in Virginia's fields,
the students as they were, myself as I was
through those ten requiems that toll me forth
to this new decade waiting to be known.
Resisted still the muskrat urge to stow
and nest and dream of calendars to come.
Distrusted still the lure of retrospect . . .
I banish now the new years with the old
and seek no future but the given day
to live my dying in the risen world.

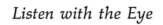

Listen with the Eye

HARLEQUINADE

Topple
from his stilts
the somersaulting dwarf,
caper to laughter,
twonk
for popcorn kids
your punchinello nose
or broom away
the pool of light
that tracks
your trampolining leaps
and falls
around the sawdust ring.

Let crowds
applaud
the first
of seven lions
whipped and chaired
through seven hoops
of flame,
or cheer
the tamer,
juggler,
death-defier,
acrobat,
equestrian,
and cycling chimpanzee.

I glory
in the everlasting bum
and bide the boring skits
until his final pantomimes
as I have bided
sleek and Dieseled
freights
to see at last
the joggled
Toonerville caboose.

Rabbled down the bleachers,
nudged toward the exit flaps,
I turn to glimpse
a gang of clowns
undo suspendered pantaloons,
detach their lightbulb
noses,
towel off their Ringling grins
and slam a wad
of trappings
into circus trunks.
Lids drop shut.
Just
like
that
the world comes back.

FLIGHT

Behind them always is
the town
diminished in departure,
a mattress rolled
and forced
into a wagon bay,
and tousled boys
papoosed
to mothers
bent and hiking
for the hope of ports.

They congregate to watch
from quiet quays
while sailors turn the capstans,
and the derricked cables
creak with rising
and descending
cargoes
cradled in a net.

Before them always
ebb away the tides
like roads that lead
and lead
from wanderings
to wonderings
where refuge and the refugee
are one,
and home is only
what you hold
and
what you are.

THE FIRST LIBERATOR

It is written in a letter in Latin
to the King of Spain from Admiral Columbus
that he landed at San Salvador,
Santa María de la Concepción, Fernandina,
Isabella, Española and Juana
on his first voyage from Palos.

It is added that on each of these islands
south of Cathay
he never saw a native clothed,
that fleet canoes propelled by seventy rowers
often tracked his ships, that native women
labored for their men, who had but one wife,
that all, except the Indians of Charis,
were liberal and loving, though timid,
sharing meat and provisions equally.
They were dark as plums but unashamed.
They hunted with spears whittled from cane
and shunned cannibalism and war.

Though his men bartered broken bottles
for the natives' pure gold and cotton,
Columbus called the king
of Navidad del Señor
his brother,
noting nonetheless that the king's land
and the land of all the islands
south of Cathay
seemed "admirably adapted for tillage,
pasture and habitation."

To safeguard which for "the holy faith of Christ"
Columbus built and garrisoned a fortress
fully armed, imploring that
"processions be made,
and sacred feasts be held,
and the temples be adorned with festive boughs . . .
in the prospect of the salvation of the souls
of so many nations hitherto lost."

At the departure of the clothed, white sailors
from San Salvador, Santa María de la Concepción,
Fernandina, Isabella, Española and Juana,
the natives waded after them
and waved their black and naked arms
or held their plum-dark children high
to see
"beings of a celestial race"
who had already taken two men
and twenty women
by force

and would return.

My Sons in God

FOR A POET WHO WRITES
AND WONDERS WHY

Because you are not what you will become
and cannot stop becoming what you are,
you never see that nothing but the lot
of being human summons you to write.

Perfect, you could know the world without a word.
Imperfect but perfectible, you must
unscroll your revelations line by line
to prove on paper what you sense at sight

as you are drawn to mirrors to confirm
that what you see reflected is yourself.
The need to be assured is nothing worse
than every poet's best apology.

Inspired, you must wait as consciously
as any actor playing dead on stage,
letting the world's quick purposes spin out
around you while you fidget with a thought

that will not let itself be brought to light
too easily or sooner than it must.
This much you owe to what the blood demands
but what the mind finds difficult to form

this side of Judgment where the mirror keeps
its darkness and the grave its victory.
Perfect as God, the final poetry
is silence, but that is still a death away.

GOD AND MAN

After casting the first act, checking sections
of scenery and mastering his rage
because the female lead blundered on page
one, he left the actors to themselves on stage
without a script and fretting for directions.

FOR MY GODSONS

Let Christ or chaos stun the world
with judgment and the final fire—
I wish you now, my sons in God,
no less than all the might of choice,
no more than Adam's cowardice
in choosing right.

Let life itself be light, and death
the dark and far of what you see.
I wish you light to parable
the dark as poets might who dare
the world from lockstep with a word
and dream it right.

Because you came to me as gifts
and now exact the manlier vows
of my godfathering, I speak
as any father might to sons
with names and blood not mine, with love
my final right.

IN THE KEY OF MIRACLES

Unseeing as an embryo, he stirred
by touching walls or windowsills and spoke
the finger conversation of the dumb.
Mornings were what he guessed at when he woke

without a clock within his silences
and fingered for his slippers near his bed.
Then—waking to one Sunday of the world
unwarned, unsure if this were how the dead

arose to glory, he saw that walls he touched
were blue, that sunslants in a rain could show
a field of stationed cows with not a cow
budging, that wind behind a rain could blow

the daisies reckless as a thousand polkas.
Stayed by the wind until the wind was gone,
he blinked the deafness from his eyes like sleep
and stared at noises, and the world went on.

FOR MY LAST CLASS OF FRESHMEN

There is no word for what I love in you,
but it is sure, sacred and daily as bread.
I speak by indirections of a world
divisible as loaves among ourselves
and multiplied like miracles because
we share the private tables of the mind.
We join in rites and sacraments that bind

and keep us bound like vows when we face God
or Plato over coffee, books and smoke.
Discovering the truth we always knew,
we look in one another's eyes surprised
and reconciled to what we shall recall
five years from now reclining on a plane,
exchanging socks, surrendering to pain,

dying or saddleblocked before a birth.
Today it is enough that we rehearse
for nothing but today and everything
abreast of us impatient to be known.
If we profess no more but nothing less,
let us be tame as eagles, mad as saints
or casual as Job in his complaints

until we learn the liturgies that sound
their psalms this second in the minstrel blood
alive from Solomon through Charlemagne
to Huckleberry's scuttlebutt to you.
Let us dare life as lovers dare the dark
and learn less stubbornly than blinded Saul
that light comes from within or not at all.

TO A BLIND STUDENT WHO
TAUGHT ME TO SEE

More reminiscent than distressed, you say
you recollect the pain of sight as I
might dream of buried men whose living hands
I shook, faces I knew, voices I heard
and hear again when I remember them.
You feel no urge to resurrect one day

when you could see a stucco chimney webbed
with rosevines, trios of basted, browning hens
revolving slowly backward on a spit,
the way a collie's torso thrust ahead
and instantly recoiled from its bark.
You claim the world is nearer in the dark.

This makes me think that Oedipus was blind
before he gouged his eyeballs from his skull.
No longer blinded by the visible,
he turned two hollow sockets on a dusk
of light he had to blind himself to see.
I draw from this that only in the mind

is there a world, and never two the same,
that blind men walk with cautious dignity
partly from need, partly because they know
the single world is multiple as men's
imaginings, that streets are nothing but
the way we picture them, that doors can shut

or open if we twist the keys or not.
Your blindness makes me memorize with you
the accidental braille of time and place
until I see how Homer saw a world
of iliads and odysseys arise
like magic to the tapping cane of thought.

I make too much of it, this matter of books
and talk and silences, but every sun
I stand less sure of what I ought to know
and find my way to them to find my way.
Wisdom's rabbit races just far enough
ahead to keep the chase invitingly close
but never done, and all I really know
is what occurs to me right here as right.
Moments of truth come anywhere at once.

Facing the jewelry of bottles twiced
by mirrors fanned behind a downtown bar
in Minneapolis, I understood a verse
from Crane's "The Wine Menagerie" without
intending it. The meaning simply *came,*
like *that*—like one of God's gratuities
that come before we are prepared. Of all
I ever worked to learn, those things are best
that came to me without my earning them.

I should have said without *deserving* them.
In Minneapolis a deeper thinker
surely would have called all truth a gift,
but it was hot, and I forgot. Later,
when students let me tell them what I knew,
I saw that all we keep of truth is what
we give away, that holocausts can sleep
like revolutions in the smallest flints,
that any river can reflect the sun.

I have a student's fear that truth is fun
to seek but death to keep. Heroes and saints
are those who freed the thoughts of God by pen
or tongue and made them last like Parthenons.
I bleed the lambs of glory for those few
who said that time must wait their christening.
Once within their presence, words take flesh,
and God wakes fires that can rock the skull
and blaze the eye with revelation.

GOAT-SONG

To bare the beast in flesh, the Greeks drew man
as satyr—waist-up human, waist-down brute.
Sculptors saw everywhere a twin of Pan,
each with the loins of a ram, some with a flute.
Not one concealed a hoof within a boot
or hid men's lowers in a business suit.
The Greeks, it seemed, preferred with rare exception
the worst distortion to the best deception.

No one imagines how the world withdrew
when she would come to me, the chained sachet
between her breasts deliberate as musk,
the drumhead of the dress around her loins
and thighs contending with the thrust of each
soft flex into the world we made and were.

Undressing, she would stand against the sun
and slip the double sling from breast and breast
until each one swayed pendant as a plum.
With skin still wrinkled where a garter left
its pressure, she would panther through the room
in nothing but her rings—and then the bath:

spilled water sliding down her tucks and folds
to heighten into bronze the brown of her
before she dabbed a towel to her parts
and rollicked on the davenport to dry.
A bitch of the streets I called her as she lay
spreadeagled near my bed and spat at books

she could not read and challenged me to slap
or wrestle her until we tossed like cats
rampaging through an Africa of hating.
Loosed of my seed, I stilled her witchery
and swore I never saw the face I saw
bewildered in the jungles of her eyes.

The sea receded fathoms at a time,
leaving the stranded porpoises to breathe
the suffocating air until they drowned.

We found them belly-up beside the sharks
and whales as if some Gulliver had gaffed
and flung them there like salmon while we slept.

No one could tell us where the ocean went
or why, or when it would come raging back.
We simply knew that we saw cavernous

horizons where a blue one used to be.
Not that we missed the drummer's roll of waves,
the jetsam on the sand, the hurricanes

that lifted rowboats to the peaks of trees
and buckled bungalows like wickerwork.
We had our fill of that but could not help

recalling sails and seascapes as they were.
When governors announced that men could walk
the ocean floor to Portugal, we felt

no urge to be the first to crush the spines
of trout beneath our boots or loot the cells
of submarines that still contained their crews.

We always thought that oceans had a right
to everything consigned to them by God
or man and never wished it otherwise.

Now we were left with decomposing crabs,
canyons of silt, mountains and continents
that no Columbus ever named or knew,

navies without a coast to guard, divers
burning their equipment, armies of scavengers,
a monumental stink from all the dead

and dying underwater life, a need
to redesign our maps, rewrite our books
and zone the bottom of the sea for sale.

TO A BICYCLIST IN FRANCE

For George James

You will mail me postcards stamped in Paris—
Notre Dame illuminée, the ferried Seine,
the usual best-foot-forward city scenes.
Saying you miss the states, your words are pure

civilian now—all rank and rancor buried
with the notes you typed from B.O.Q.'s another
breed ago. You left the generals
their jeeps and crew-cuts for a biker's tour

of Europe on your saved-up pay, and shunned
the niche your father wanted you to fit . . .
The ex-lieutenant in me wakes and shakes
me ten years back. I could have hiked from Caen,

have cashed my bonds and severance for fare
and pedaled humming through Montmartre, Versailles,
Provençe and downward to Marseilles, but I
had someone else to be with somewhere next

to go with something there to do. My past
leaves Europe still mere names to me. At times
I have regrets—replot alternatives
I could have lived—pronounce my lived years lost . . .

Yet I can write without a hint of cant
I ride with you across the fact of France
as fast as I can think since thinking takes
me where I am despite these accidents

of place. Paris by night and Pittsburgh hills
are similarly still at 4:00 A.M.
Stillness is stillness, life is life, and earth
remains the earth with days quite short, and nights

shorter, and trips the shortest prank of chance.
Apart, we breathe this day alike and stand
an equal distance from eternity—
you there in the U.S.A., me here in France.

DYING UNDER DRILLING

Staring at a dentist's upside-down face, I tongue
the sand of pumice from my gums. "Rinse out."
I swill. "Open." I yawn like a baying wolf
at moons of frosted, incandescent bulbs.
More picks and clamps—a twang of snapping floss—
green spray that cools like winds of peppermint.
Beside me on a shelf, a skull—teeth clenched
in gumless glee or fury—hard to tell.
Who was this man? In heaven now, or hell?

When Hamlet stared at Yorick's dug-up grin,
did he consider anything beyond
mortality? Did he presume as I
assume that teeth are singular as souls
and fingerprints, that bodies burned to soot
can still be known as George or Josephine
by one identifying molar? Now,
updated by contraptions, a regress
to years when Mohawks practiced for distress

by letting chieftains hammer good bicuspids
out. In lesser anguish, David ordered
God to crush within their jaws the teeth
of all his enemies. But Mohawk guts
are dust with David's bones. Moldering now
like Hamlet stymied by a skull, I age
toward the buried Yorick I will be,
and, needled numb with darts of novocain,
I fence with pain before the end of pain.

THE MIDDLE OF THE WORLD

Call it the dark wood's year. Call it a year
of hell and mountains and a guide to keep
at bay the leopard, lion and the wolf.
Call it something! I am ripe for parables.
My only mountain is the one I climb
to work, and I am tired of climbing it.
The up-and-downing mornings slash and cut

to dust my threescore years and ten. Divide
by two, and here I stop. Midway and rushed,
I keep what I started with: my father's name,
my mother's eyes, righthanded ways with forks,
pencils, fights and good handshakes, no real
philosophy of pain, a few vague doubts
in God, some fear of death and no regrets.

In similar darkness Dante searched for peace
from devil's ice to stars. Today I smirk
at years when men could rhyme their way to God
as they could love, beget and die on the same
mattress. I have no tooth for comedy,
and there is hell enough on earth to jar
me loose from poetry for life. I fear

God's underlings who damn the innocent
and kill the merciful. If I could climb
from zero to the holy peak, I still
would say that any sparrow's fall defines
the yea of heaven and the nay of hell.
I rhyme no answers from the cold and far.
I ask no more than starlight from a star.

MIDNIGHT PIPE

I tamp tobacco in my pipe and flare
a match to it and blur the bedroom air
with smoke that curls in layers to the light.
I find I cannot smoke without some light.
The taste of tongue must match the taste of sight
for me regardless of the time of night.

My heart thuds blind against its jail of bone.
I feel it while I hold this blackened stone
of briar in my palm—the punctual blood
aflow since God breathed Adam out of mud
and sailed the risk of Noah through the flood.
I time three smoke-rings to the tock of blood

and think of old Mark Twain who puffed a cob
the night he died as if he meant to rob
the thief who waited by his bed of one
persisting relish from the past of men . . .
I rack my pipe and wait and wonder when
I will breathe out and never in again.

COUNTERCLOCK

The world begins when I begin
blinking awake on sheets that night
and marriage have reduced to knots.
Asleep, my wife postpones the sun
and what its burning means to me—
compulsions of the body, soap-
juice in a washrag, razorwork.

Five years ago, ten years ago
the same deeds waited to be done
no differently at sun o'clock.
I woke to ceilings low or high
but always strange in Washington,
New York, Chicago, Saranac,
Quebec, Virginia Beach, Lejeune

and waited for the night before
to jell and tell me where I was.
I do the same thing now, hoping
my mind will flex as surely as
my fingers on the mattress edge,
but nothing in the room turns real.
I sense a stranger in myself,

a stranger in the sleeping girl
I chose a life away from here,
a strangeness in the house, the air.
I stare at walls like Lazarus
or Rip Van Winkle, mystified
because I cannot right myself
by linking now with yesterday.

The trick I learned of thinking back
to go ahead keeps breaking down
until the only thing I know
is that I am a man awake
and turning with the turning world
in this year's ring around the sun.
When collies bark across the street

and lure me to the windowsill
to see that snow is snow, sky sky
and milkmen sanctified by sun
where not a clock can shadow them,
I see all over what I saw
but never saw while it is now
and always yesterday today.

THE CLEAVING

Imagining my wife dead, I am stopped,
stilled, halved and driven singly back to fears
too real for loneliness alone to name.
Then, nothing. Slowly intimidations shame

me back and up from hell like Orpheus,
saying *it was not time, it was not time*
to leave her rouged and coffined for the dead
still left alive to see. I learn instead

that death in dreams or out of dreams is loss
enough to stun my waking like a wheel
left spun and spinning from an accident.
But while I wonder what it means or meant,

I think of Orpheus who charmed the king
of hell and calmed the tortures of the damned
with songs just long enough to find his wife
again and lead her by the hand to life

until he lost her twice. What lover mocks
the lot of Orpheus who dared the gods
and bearded them for someone else's sake?
With nothing but a dead girl's life at stake

he sang her to the stars before he faltered,
panicked and let her go. The myth survives.
The fear of loss is every lover's hell.
Remember Orpheus and how he fell.

FIRST WILL AND TESTAMENT

Stripped of my trousers, shirt and downtown coat,
I stall the stalemate of the year to lounge
in undershorts and chew an applehalf.
Bombers are right now armed and in the air
while tulips spear and fountain into rows.
Without the worsted armor of my clothes

I rise as free as oxygen and let
no other meddlers but the miracles
of tulips slip the radar of my sight.
I live in cold-war Easter, seamed in skin
but willed by resurrection to survive
this world that waits for bombers to arrive.

Headlines from tomorrow's garbage paper say
Russians are walling in or walling out
the Germans brick by checkpoint on a map.
Tulips will freeze by forecast late tonight.
Tan generals are warning of the worst
and stressing that the Russians still are first

at boomeranging men around the earth.
Defeat, the headlines of defeat repeat
the massacres, the tests, the incidents
that could unloose the bombs to bloom in flame
and snow the sentenced hemispheres with dust.
Trapped by the guilt of Judas and the lust

of Cain, I force myself to think that war
will never come, that we shall live in peace
to face disease, old age or sudden death
as quietly as tulips brace for frost,
that I might never tell as Matthew told
of Christ how every risen day was sold

with each new Eden of my traitor's breath.
But I am bone of Judas, blood of Cain.
I wash my hands of what might yet be done
and wait the world's fierce end by sitting still
with nothing but a core and cotton brief,
updating Adam's bite, and Adam's leaf.

PITTSBURGH IN PASSING

Between old battles and the ones I should
be seeing, I have lost my circus eyes.
Birthdays are deathdays. I feel the glaciering
of centuries beneath the pulse of clocks
and through the blown-out candles of my blood.

I stand unarmed where Braddock's armies stood.
Instead of Hurons I see acres piped
and sewered for our waste and mined with bones
of Quakers, Indians and immigrants.
Three decades in the woods of William Penn

have left me kin to all the buried men
who claimed this wilderness and named this town.
Where Washington marched in buckskin, I can drive
through battlefields of signs and ironworks,
inhale unrevolutionary air

and damn the siren waking me to war-
alerts each Monday of the year. Senates
have bolstered us with bunkercaves and rockets.
A palisade of missiles rings the town
while banking and burlesque thrive back to back

in the same building. Threats of surprise attack
would bench a naked tease and the most correct
of tellers flank to flank in a joint shelter.
No one objects. Shielded around the clock
by minutemen in radar shacks, we tomb

the Hiroshima world beside old Rome
and older Troy while mayors fatten us
with talk. No one admits we walk on skulls,
and no one prays Isaiah back to speak
the truth without refining it to please!

The siren spins. The aborigines
and whites who battled here are six wars old.
Chained to a different blunderbluss, we sleep
in cemeteries screened by warhead forts
and dream our moats are still the seven seas.

Agreed—that God created just so many stones
to be until the end of things, letting them spread
by splitting under lightning and the avalanche
of sledging rain or simply lasting in a world
of all that multiplies and serves its term and dies.

Boarding the airport bus behind the U.S. Mint,
I found a stone no rounder than a rundown dime
and thumbed it warm against the pocket of my palm.
It still was stone when men on mountains spoke to God
or when I last took off from Truman's Washington

by DC-6 and never thought of coming back.
A similar, different man on similar, different streets,
I did return to find what turned all clocks to toys.
Knowing in part within the always known to God,
I tried to probe my more-than-animal but less-

than-angel past before I heard my flight announced.
Ten years had given me less willingness to die,
more lustfire in the chest, more singular a need
to leave mementos more than bones to stoke my grave.
Simple in its perfect death, the stone I gripped defied

those years that made me die a little to survive
to new departures from an older terminal.
Later, at fourteen thousand feet above the rocks
of Maryland, I dreamed of death again and fought
to think of something else by watching clouds as bare

and beautiful as untouched snow or studying
the adequate backside of either stewardess.
Nothing would work, and there was nothing I could say
to still that timebomb-stone created to outlast
the turbo-jet that battled gravity to climb

on schedule over Arlington—the ring of roads
around the target-town of presidents, parades,
hoteling clans, continuous burlesque and cabs—
the self I had to save from trying stonily to spite
what cramped my hand and heart until I let it go.

ELIZABETH RIVER FERRY

Tranced by the chasing wake, I thought how right
were those first Greeks who dreamed a ferry best
to sail dead souls toward the farthest world.
A faster ship could churn the black waves white.

A slower one could raft boatman, crew and all
like so much driftwood past the ports of hell.
No neated metaphor could match the night
we left the Portsmouth backwash to the gulls

that circled tattoo parlors, barracks, saloons,
two sailors shooting craps against a curb
and blondes in a Ford with leopardskin decor.
Honking a low klaxon, we keeled through moons

and reefs of neon flashed from Norfolk lights
until we neared the Norfolk docks and saw
barracks, saloons, SP's with white brassards,
two sailors shooting craps against a crate,

blondes in a Cadillac with zebra decor
and tattooed yeomen spitting at a tire
clamped like a buffer to the ramming prow.
Jostled from schemes to parable those shores,

I watched the swill and whirlpools by the pier
submerge mythology while klaxons struck,
dice bounced, blondes sucked at private cigarettes
as if no one had solved the world before

white navigators brought their arsenals
to claim this river for Elizabeth
and dreamed new myths to civilize the sea
with fleets that sailed as sure as funerals.

The runover fox receding in the rear-
view mirror of my mind refocuses
a world I knew by name before it changed.
Now mountains are more present than they were.
Rivers are fiercely rivers and belie
blue veins in superscript across a map.
Horses seem strange and yet so strangely real
I cannot bear to look at them for long.
Baffled, I must relearn the universe
as children learn the words for animals
by matching pictures to a line of print.

If there are meanings in a smear of pelt
and wild blood upon a road, I swear
these meanings break and re-create the mind.
They rally from revivals and arise
like men from underwater fear who bite
back all their breath before they reach the waves
and lunge for eucharists of sun and wind.
If promenading lovers claim by day
they never felt the night's surrendering
submerge their flesh in silences more still
and still more eloquent than requiems,

I prophesy before the jealous Lord
of mountains, rivers, horses and the first
of Eden's kisses that such lovers lie.
A silence rises from the death of flesh
that trumpets down all Jerichos of fact
and leaves us strangers in a land we claim.
So does the world dissemble in the blood
of God and somehow still remain the world.
It waits redemptions that are man's to give
from now until the land and waters burn
and four dark horses rage beneath the sun.

Blood Rights

CIRCLING

Closer, I might see what water does
to rocks, and rocks to water—might read
the names of tugs diverging to the compass
points on Flushing Bay like gnats

across the skin of ponds. Instead,
I study cloudfoam and mountaintides
fogged in like cardboard country under
bunting. From twenty thousand feet

the Bronx conforms to abstract paintings
of the Bronx in atlases. Westward, Manhattan
sizzles like a grid of O's and X's
in a clash of tactics. Nearer, I might

scrutinize a tamer's lion gorged
with ox—drivers with lockjaw faces—
newsrack strippers showing this and that
to queues of browsers—books collapsing

on a shelf like sentinels who topple
from attention at attention. Stacked up
on this Olympus like a god, I see
no more than gray peninsulas and crisscross

roads. Round and around. No wonder
Zeus preferred sealevel living
to his alpy throne. Bollixed with altitude,
that old rapscallion's blood demanded

wenching in Salonika or sea-chilled wine
or anything to break his high monotony.
Divine or damned, the blood demands
a landing. Better to risk the earth

than drone in zeros. Better to breathe
the grubby air where every day
is worth the waking. Godfather, show
no where to walk. I'll have to gamble

catching hell in heaven if I stumble.

My boys, we lied to you.
The world by definition stinks
of Cain, no matter what
your teachers told you. Heroes
and the fools of God may rise
like accidental green
or gray saharas, but the sand
stays smotheringly near.

Deny me if you can. Already
you are turning into personnel,
manpower, figures on a list
of earners, voters, prayers,
soldiers, payers, sums
of population tamed with forms:
last name, middle name, first name—
telephone—date of birth—

home address—age—hobbies—
experience. Tell them the truth.
Your name is Legion. You
are aged a million. Tell
them that. Say you breathe
between appointments: first day,
last day. The rest is no
one's business. Boys, the time

is prime for prophecy.
Books break down their bookends.
Paintings burst their frames.
The world is more than reason's
peanut. Homer sang it real.
Goya painted it, and Shakespeare
staged it for the pelting rinds
of every groundling of the Globe.

Wake up! Tonight the lions
hunt in Kenya. They
can eat a man. Rockets
are spearing through the sky.
They can blast a man to nothing.
Rumors prowl like rebellions.
They can knife a man. No one
survives for long, my boys.

Flesh is always in season,
lusted after, gunned, grenaded,
tabulated through machines,
incinerated, beaten to applause,
anesthetized, autopsied, mourned.
The blood of Troy beats on
in Goya's paintings and the truce
of Lear. Reason yourselves

to that, my buckaroos,
before you rage for God,
country and siss-boom-bah!
You won't, of course. Your schooling
left you trained to serve
like cocksure Paul before
God's lightning smashed
him from his saddle. So—

I wish you what I wish
myself: hard questions
and the nights to answer them,
the grace of disappointment
and the right to seem the fool
for justice. That's enough.
Cowards might ask for more.
Heroes have died for less.

COUNTDOWN

Kneeling at groundzero,
pilgrims are kissing bright
the bolted star where Christ
first breathed in Bethlehem.
Upstairs, a priest passes
a dish for coppers he will pocket.

Eleusis, Mecca, Rome . . .
Each revelation breeds
believers and a shrine
where Chaucer's pardoner
can pawn the "pigges bones"
of hope. I've had enough

of this museum-faith
that sucks on history.
A birth or death can happen
anywhere. Why monument
a saving accident
or date the centuries

from Christ's or anybody's
coming? Let the hawkers
work or starve. I choose
the odds that stay at odds
with memory. Under
the warhead sky, the cities

bloom with dandelion
shrines to martyrs, riots,
battles, concentration camps,
assassinations, guilt.
Displays in Hiroshima
show one bomb's effect

on hair and bottle caps
preserved, identified
and mounted on a board
like moths. For what? Who needs
memorials to prove
that all the years add up

to now, that nowhere needs
remembering but here?
The joke's on God. Defenders
of His name are counting down
to zero and the last ascensions.
The dead keep burying the dead.

BATTLE NEWS

For breakfast—war and coffee. Pilots
have been downed like skeet, and captives,
tortured in a tub or booted in the groin
until they talked. A Cardinal approves
of troop morale. His speech before

the V.F.W. is reproduced beneath
the photo of a sergeant burned in error.
After three wars, I should be numb
to every morning's muster of the dead.
The Cardinal seems numb enough. He preached

a twin address the year I swore
to fight all foreign and domestic
enemies with nothing but my hands, so help
me God. When I marched home, I might
have told his Eminence, "Don't

talk pluralities to me. I breathe
alone and so do you, and one
times one was never more than one.
The smallest pin of pain can show
that one umtillionth of the world

is not the name that anybody answers to."
I never breathed a word, and now the daily
death count booked between the weather
and the baseball scores leaves nothing new
to say. The cost remains numerical,

the order, alphabetical. Only the spellings
change from war to war. Between
the lines I think of aborigines
who would not touch their wives or eat
until they had atoned for every

enemy they speared in battle. Justice
or no justice, shall no one say
that hunters rove the earth from now
to heaven? Who cares if men in diving
suits are swimming to the moon like sperm?

They're out for battlefields where flying
armies shall dispute the stars. I know
it's militarily absurd to claim that life
means more than trying not to die,
but if it does, what then? What now?

A SPARROW'S WORTH OF FEAR

Rainbows of gasoline on puddletops
riddle the puddled sun with lavenders
and greens. Submerged, a sparrow molders where
it plunged, its legs tucked in like landing gear
between a quiet cross of wings. I wrap
it in a shroud of headlines, stow it deep
in rubbish, lid the tomb. My fingers keep

remembering the feel of wings that soared
from gutters to the southern seas and—. Boom!
Windthump and motorsock collide and pump
like gunshot after gunshot in a hangar. Jarred,
the waterlily sun dissolves in ripples.
Jets zoom by, unraveling pure trails
of vapor spoored in thunder from their tails.

The trees explode with sparrows. Jostled branches
chime in place like carillons. Now, calm.
Now, sediment. The sun returns its bullseye
on the rainbow slime. The birds perch cold
as taxidermy in the trees. The world
becomes the sparrow's land it was before
it shuddered to the drum of some day's war.

Of some day's war . . . The words unlock the winds.
While anyone is burying a bird
or naming colors in a pool, a plane
could soar across the sun and leave us blown
to dust and shadowed by its crucifix.
Then, calm. Then, sediment. Then, sun returning
over nothing but remains and rubbish, burning.

I am all head like a trout observed
straight-on. This fish-face has mooned
at me before from polished doorknobs:
Cyclops—single-eyed but double-nosed.

"Advance." My head soars gothically
until it mushrooms where the glass bends:
atomic Hazo. "Retreat." Cyclops again.
"Face right." My head shrinks to a bean

on trousered stilts. "Face about."
I sprout a ball-belly, rocking
like a balloon that will always land
on duck-feet. To hell with tricks.

Give me a flat glass that lets me count
my whiskers, preen and pat myself
with talc and stare at eyeballs staring
back. I spot it like an old assurer

on a globe that bowls a thousand worlds
of bubble gum. "Grin back, old twin."
What lives in wonderland dies fast.
The bubble of the world is waiting.

THE SUN RUNNER

The swirls and metronomes of watersprays
condemn the afternoon like oxen yoked
and sentenced to a well. Lightyears away,
the sun explodes without a sound and stays

deadcenter in the sky. Nothing takes flight,
and nothing walks while every sprinkler clocks
my blood to dust again. I want to run
the hills in one straight line and out of sight,

pacing the summits like the Indians
of Lima who could race twelve hundred miles
in ten successive days across Peru.
I see them loping like Olympians

by sun and star, leaving the conquered fords
and mountains to their own eternity.
But this is Pittsburgh, U.S.A. No one
remembers Indians except as hordes

pursued by cavalry on two square feet
of glass in fifty million dens a day . . .
With sun and shadow in pursuit, I sprint
like some lean Inca down the treadmill street.

The lawns are burning to a golden death.
Sunbathers sit decaying in their swings.
Between the gauntlet-houses matched like graves,
I run until I have to stop for breath.

NIJINSKY IN ST. MORITZ

I am a madman with sense and my nerves are trained.
from his *Diary*

Ask anyone. The cannibals are here
and everywhere. They eat whole men alive,
though not by mouth. Mouths savor
pigfat, bullflank, chickenskin . . .
Eyes are more ravenous. Insatiable,
they steadily devour matadors,
saviors, nudes or kings like meat
flung to piranhas. And human ears
have fangs. They can reduce a man
to powder just by listening.

Why frown? What, my fellow sacrifice,
could be more natural? Infants
eat their mothers. Lovers relish lovers.
I have been swallowed by Diaghilev,
my wife, my daughter and the doctors.
Unnatural? Then, everything's unnatural. God's
supper is Himself, and everyone is God.
Deny it if you can before you say
I'm mad. Don't look so damn insulted.
The cannibals are here. I'm one. You're one.

A NUDE FOR EITHER EYE

1

Her body is the raised baton
that taps the resting sketchers back
to easels, palettes, paints and her.
A scar from belly surgery

tucks in as she reseats herself
sidesaddle on a sheeted stool
and stops. The pose and body fuse.
The mold of holding merely still

recedes, recedes. Slowly her eyes
repeal the glaze of some unstaring
statuette to leave revealed
only a woman in repose

without her clothes. Aloof, alone,
with nothing showing but her skin,
she keeps concealed like breath or bone
the real and second nude within.

2

These names, this fraudulence . . .
A model, nude and necklaced on a sheet,
can beckon kings or saviors to her loins
with zingo eloquence.

Ponder how beauty lets
its lovers blunder while it drums the blood.
Whatever makes us tune its silences
aloud with alphabets

escapes by pulsing on
for blunderers to miss the measure of,
lending itself to wonder like a girl
necklaced, with nothing on.

THE YEAR THE GIRLS WENT NAKED

Interest was immediate. Interviewed,
girls hid nothing. Nipples stared
like animal eyes, unblinking. Bellies
were bellies. Ungirdled buttocks
spread more, stuck to leather

and skinned to a burn if brushed
in passing. Tourism instantly boomed,
but garmentmakers closed within
a week. Ditto: cosmeticians, cleaners,
launderers, fashion salons and, oddly,

brothels. In ninety days *voyeur*
passed from usage, surviving only
in journals, crosswords and dictionaries.
A year to the day few children under
ten remembered how to sketch a dress.

Breast cancer ebbed to negligible
percentages. Burlesque's revival
peaked when pre-strippers ended
their routines voluptuously gloved,
stockinged, gowned and shod. Bankrupt

pornographers went on relief.
Faced with unemployment, rapid
decline in the birthrate, and gradual
malaise ascribed to sexual indifference,
all governors and clergy preached crusades.

Offenders were threatened with "public
dressings." Punishments ensued. Desire
returned to normal, stabilizing crime,
churchgoing, psychoanalysis, commerce,
advertising, nightlife and other sublimations.

[84]

THE DELILAH INCIDENT

I've read the *Book of Judges,*
studied *Samson Agonistes,*
seen Cecil B. DeMille's
protracted technicolor bunk
of the event.
                I'm not impressed.
Granted, Delilah was a vamp
of some distinction. Granted,
her lips were full; her breasts,
exaggerated to entice;
her wine, stronger than usual;
her lutes, hypnotic, and her scissors,
sharp. Granted, too, that Samson
let himself be duped and doped
until he sprawled asleep
like some exhausted spaniel
on her lap.
             But why ascribe
such hooey to a haircut?
Why join the centuries of suckers
who believe without a clue
of logic, proof or precedent
that Samson really lost his muscle
with his curls?
             My guess remains
that he awoke, observed his sideburns
on the floor and said with some
annoyance to the wench, "What made

you do a thing like that?"
When she responded with a laugh
and clapped for bodyguards, he flung
her in the swimming pool, slugged
the waiters with a table, told
the guards in Hebrew where
to go and left the premises.

TWILIGHT IN ST. PETERSBURG

Octogenarians from York,
Poughkeepsie, Cleveland, Baltimore
and Broken Arrow, Oklahoma,
littered their canes, carts and wheelchairs
on the porch of the Ponce de Leon
Hotel. Turning from jigsaw puzzles
spilled on tables set for solitaire,

they watched the stone angel in the lobby
pee eight quarts of Tampa Bay
per minute in an everlasting stream.
Only the lobby cat ignored
the splash. He slept St. Peter's sleep,
inverted on the stairs, his paws outspread,
his nine lives purring in the dying air.

THE END

The curtain stuck, leaving
the couple who had played the scene
stranded in character and forced
to exit as themselves. They crossed

offstage in opposite directions
like lovers unexpectedly surprised
and shamed apart—the mood
shattered, the feeling lost.

A CANDLE FROM PETRA

For Ibrahim Tawil

This thing? A Nabatean lamp
that poets stemmed with oiled wicks
and fired when they wrote by night.
A thousand kings ago, this light

ignited over parchments quilled
with script in Arabic until
crusaders watched it drown in sand.
No one can shake the digger's hand

that shook this lamp against his palm
and saw the hourglassing sand
and scorpion spill out, and no
one in Arabia can know

the bedouin who wicked it once
for burning. Now, this ounce of clay
seems hardly worth the match to flame
it by. I keep it just to claim

attention for an Arab gowned
against the wind and pondering
what makes a poet wake at night
to search for paper and some light.

NO ECHO IN JUDEA

As I drive south to Christ and Abraham
the tires speed the desert road before
me back to Syria. The clocks have stopped.
Only the sky turns modern when a jet
veers eastward for Bombay. Below
its powered wings stand sheep and bedouin.

The sun blinks at me from a donkey's eye
exactly as it blinked eight centuries
ago on tribes of Arabs armed to purge
the last crusader from Jerusalem.
How many bones survive? How many skulls
did Timurlane leave stacked in pyramids

where bedouin fork wheat against the wind
and watch it fall. I squint for evidence.
The deadness of the sea near Jericho
unscrolls no secrets, and the sand endures
for wind alone to sift and re-arrange
and blow the smell of Briton, Frenchman, Turk

and Mongol to the sun. The time is what
it was when Sarah laughed the angel back
to God. The shepherds wait for Christ. The tribes
of Canaan graze their camels near the road
I conquer like a new crusader armed
with film and cigarettes. Nursed on the blood

of Europe's cross and Europe's rack, I search
for what was here before the world moved west.
A donkey blinks. Bedouin cane their sheep.
A child cries until his mother plumps
her breast against him, thumbs the nipple firm
and plugs the blind mouth mute as history.

FOR FAWZI IN JERUSALEM

Leaving a world too old to name
and too undying to forsake,
I flew the cold, expensive sea
toward Columbus' mistake
where life could never be the same

for me. In Jerash on the sand
I saw the colonnades of Rome
bleach in the sun like skeletons.
Behind a convalescent home,
armed soldiers guarded no man's land

between Jordanians and Jews.
Opposing sentries frowned and spat.
Fawzi, you mocked in Arabic
this justice from Jehoshophat
before you shined my Pittsburgh shoes

for nothing. Why you never kept
the coins I offered you is still
your secret and your victory.
Saying you saw marauders kill
your father while Beershebans wept

for mercy in their holy war,
you told me how you stole to stay
alive. You must have thought I thought
your history would make me pay
a couple of piastres more

than any shine was worth—and I
was ready to—when you said, "No,
I never take. I never want
America to think I throw
myself on you. I never lie."

I watched your young but old man's stare
demand the sword to flash again
in blood and flame from Jericho
and leave the bones of these new men
of Judah bleaching in the air

like Roman stones upon the plain
of Jerash. Then you faced away.
Jerusalem, Jerusalem,
I asked myself if I could hope
for peace and not recall the pain

you spoke. But what could hoping do?
Today I live your loss in no
man's land but mine, and every time
I talk of fates not just but so,
Fawzi, my friend, I think of you.

THE BLACK LANCER

For Vassilis Vassilikos

How many eels and dolphins swerved
beneath his arms
before the mermen glimpsed
a nude king with a beard of iron
braided—a spear bannered with plankton—
the pitted eyes sighting, and the loins,
as he hurled, more sinewed than a lion's?

His toes in the Aegean shoals
tramped kingdoms down
until the grappling ropes
discovered him, and he arose.
His spear surrendered to the jaws
of sharks but left his hand still shaped
around a shape no longer lancing. Roped

to the sun, Poseidon's torso flowed
with night and burned
within itself like coal.
The eyes, the eyes hurled javelins
at living stones and dying men
who still could trample death and sing
and burn in resurrection like a king.

WAITING IN ISTANBUL

Extend this pause for years, for life. Never
to hear a Turk announce in English, French
and German that my plane will jet non-stop
for the United States. I shall not see
my country or my countrymen. Mornings
will ditto—sun by sun—the dawn before.
The newlyweds from Spain shall telescope
each other with a Leica. Ataturk's
memorials will gleam from banners furled
like flags above the gates and call the world

to witness. Purposes stalled, what will I do?
Condemn the zero-clock? Be satisfied to walk
and multiply the cube of six by six
by six until I blunder? Bargain with clerks
who prate like Finns or Magyars while they hawk
brass knives or meerschaum pipes to passengers?
Turn philosophical and say that life
means more than motion even in a land
where thieves could lose their wrists in punishment?
Or learn why Romeo feared banishment

far more than death? In lavatories stained
with butts and urine, I surprise the face
of exiles in my own. Trapped in a stall,
a janitor sits cramping out his stools.
The paper he will use shows photographs
of marching Turks and dynamited Greeks.
Slouching, he grins like Charon back from Styx
or Goya's Saturn, slavering the blood
of sons. I breathe like someone in a well.
Is this the time it always is in hell?

THE LAST BREATH

You choke while I am reading Xenophon.
Hemorrhage and history. I try to find
the link. Intent upon her purposes,
a nurse leans starchily to clock your pulse.
Limp as a hanged man's, your fingers twitch and drop
and slow my thinking down to now. Tomorrow

slips like smoke across a windowsill. Who let
the world go? I've lost my place. The past zigzags
from sentences to words to gibberish.
I hardly know the men named you and me.
So, Xenophon is right. Breathe day by day.
Survive. Let continuity be damned.

Before the last hangmen, what will it mean
if we walked boulders warmed by Christ's own feet,
talked Shakespeare while the Avon flowed with swans
and rented skiffs, saw half of Europe green
below the clouds below a Comet's wing
or watched a pair of hornets tread the soft

black bruises of dropped peaches? Concede the plot
to God. Right now the only time is breath,
and time is running out. You try your last
to breathe the clock away before the nurses
shroud you like a dollar's worth of chemicals—
parenthesized—no longer in the script.

INTENSIVE CARE

Restricted, sterile as a nursery,
the hallfloor insulates my steps.
A nurse strides by as only
nurses can, sure
of herself, sure of her shoes.

At every door I half-
expect to see new babies
blanketed in tipped-up cribs
instead of bodies tapped
by catheters. One man

is terminal. His heartcount
blinks and scrawls itself
across a monitor. He
whispers to a nurse, "I'm
dying naked." Arranging

him, she shapes his pillow
as she would an infant's
while the blinks diminish
beat by beat, then down
a beat, then less. Drowning,

he sinks alive beneath
his sedatives and waits
without a tremor for his inner
murderer to pick his time
and strike. My symptoms match.

An alien to every element,
I wait for fates that wait
to finish me. Too near,
I'll burn. Too deep,
I'll burst. Too high,

I'll choke. Too old,
I'll sicken to a final
infancy. Each breath is my
reprieve, and each reprieve,
the name of my re-sentencing.

FOR MY AUNT KATHERINE
AFTER MIDNIGHT

The hall of mirrors in my skull
repeats you everywhere I look
until I break like glass and reach
for doorknobs, radios, a coin
of searock blown by seawind smooth
as fingertips. The nights turn long.

Unable to unthink, I lug
the cross of my own mind in search
of any word to breathe against
the dark. The only word is breath,
and that is still a night away
from what you are. That near. That far.

CHILD OF OUR BODIES

Midway to birth, you are your own
secret. No one can tell me
how you'll be or when or where . . .

Not that the universe will change.
Suspended in the wombing air
where everything begins, the earth

keeps rolling on its ring from sun
to moon to sun again. I've sailed
the circle almost forty times,

but now your future makes me live
a different present than the one
I lived before you happened. Yes,

happened! After eleven years
my only precedent is silence.
I wait the justice of your eyes

exactly as I'm waiting now
for words to say what waiting means.
It does no good to school myself

for possibilities. Between
what never was and what shall be,
the only bravery is innocence.

THE FATHERING

My boy sleeps crucified.
Beside his outflung arms
stand guard a poodle
and a polkadot giraffe

completely blind to his
prefiguring. I say,
"Today's too soon
for sentencing the innocent.

Give him some time.
Give him some time.
Let yesterday's reminders
wait until he arms

himself for God knows what."
As usual, my timing's
off. The script's been cast.
We breathe in character—

five-month-old father,
five-month-old son—
split by generations,
bound by blood rights

and a watcher's worth
of promises. For bread,
I will not give him
stones. For fish, I will

not offer him a snake.
But what shall wake him when
I sleep—what mobs, what
clubs, what chalices?

MIDWAY TO MIDNIGHT

In Melbourne it's tomorrow
  while it's still six hours
  after yesterday in Anchorage.
No matter.
          Each time I look
  at you I know it's now
  and everywhere this minute—
  this minute on the Rue Benoit,
  this minute in the tower
  of Salonika, this very minute
  in Tobruk, this minute here
  in quiet Capricorn where I
  spoon out your custard from a jar.
Noon o'clock.
          Zoo-bears
  are stirring.
          The coughs of lions
  peal and volley from their pits
  like muted howitzers.
          Aloof,
  a prince of a pheasant lets
  the lawn support him while he struts
  his harem.
          You're not concerned.
Under the flashbulb-sun
  you sleep toward tonight
  while, now by now, the present
  becomes the present becomes
  the present.

A junk is sinking
in the China Sea.
Lovers
are nearing for a kiss along
the Via Maura . . .
Wake when you please,
my son.
A lion fangs
his beef.
The lovers kiss.
The world keeps happening.

From books and campuses I grew
    to learn the strategy of sharks.
I'm of the generation schooled
    for peace, then trained to murder
Abel after Abel trained
to murder me.
                    Who cares?
Who stops to prophesy?
                    Isaiah
    died a different law
ago.
        Ezekiel is just
a name.
        Dead Jeremiah will not
rise.
        Nations behave like
bourgeois wives with nothing
else to do but wait to be
offended.
            No matter where I am,
the picture sickens me.
                    I wake
to walk it off . . .
            In 1953
I woke to walk these same
fishmarket streets.
            Korea
in a headline tossed and tumbleweeded
down the Mason-Dixon docks
toward the bay.

I'd seen
my share of starched monotonies
of khaki.
I'd learned how rank
and uniforms could shrink
their wearers.
"Bodies to count
and boss,"a one-eyed captain
told me, "That's all an army
means."
His missing eye
kept weeping as he spoke.
The other zeroed in serenely
on my target-face and froze
it in the gunsight of his mind . . .
Tonight he leans across the years,
his hunter's squint still
sniping from the turret
of his skull.
I'd like to say,
"Old salt, old gunner, what's
become of you?
Who wears
the cap you crested like a fin
to cleave the wind?
Remember
me?
I'm one among the ditto
looies you prepared for glory . . ."
My only listeners are barrels
brimmed with shrimp.

                              Beside
      a capstan splotched with pigeon
      lime and barnacles of gum,
      I stop where land stops.
                              The sea
      sails level to the sky.
But underneath that calm, what
      wars, what counterparts?
                              Silent
      in sharkwater, the nearly blind
      and brainless killers scavenge
      for blood and targets.
                              Nothing
      diverts them.
                        They've stayed
      the same since God.
                              They breed
      their own majorities.
                              They last.

SWIM

Behind my shoulders now
  the hanging moss of swings,
  popcorn, babies urinating
  through their bathing trunks,
  and dunes where couples later
  by the moon shall lie and lock
  in love's pretzel—.
             Seashore,
  I take leave of you for waves
  that surge like ink beyond
  the warning buoys.
             Farther,
  where the ink turns gray, turns
  green, turns purple to the sun,
  a submarine pumps out its bilges,
  veers and noses cleanly
  as a shark for Newport News.
Downcurrent, porpoises contort
  and gleam and vanish . . .
             There . . .
The combers ride behind
  me, ride and slacken
  back to surf and leave me be.
The lifeguard's whistle skips
  across the water like a stone,
  but I swim out and dare
  a cramp to knife me down
  to God.
             Later, I will seem
  the world's first fool,
  but now I judge myself
  by what I'm willing to survive
  without.

The beach means nothing
but a pound of folded clothing
checked for a chip I've rung
around my wrist.
                    Billfold,
keys to a door, the gathered
cards of my identity recede
like tides.
                    I'm just deadweight
bob-bobbing on the ballast
of my lungs that cannot choose
but float me eastward
from Virginia.
                    My fingerfaces
shrink with salt, but I
reach out for distance
and the time when all this sea
shall wear me down to man.
I want to crave each breath
until I feel what breathing
means.
                    My arms must ache,
my blood must burn before
I stroke ashore from outright
need and drop facedown
beneath the towel of the wind
and smell the sunset in a blanket.

Under covers under ceiling
   under sky, I'm up.
                    My eyes
   are wide awake behind
   their eyelid-skins, and I
   can see for years in all
   directions.
                    What's left
   of me?
                    Student, trucker,
   captain, teacher, doctor
   of philosophy, professor, dean—
   how many titles have I
   hid behind?
                    From such a wreck
   of roles, who knows what led
   me to myself on August
   on the Rue Jacob.
                    My feet
   were absolutely under me.
I spoke that minute
   what I knew that minute.
My head was mine—not merely
   Hazo's or American, but mine
   as flesh and breath are mine . . .
Tonight, at home, I rove
   the Paris of my mind—scornful
   of clocks, uncrucified
   by longitudes and latitudes,
   no longer just the name
   at this address.
                    Eyes-open,
   eyelids-shut, I let

the truth of walls possess me
like a pulse.
                    Each thing
is namelessly itself while,
all around me, names
reject the world.
                    Non-violence
is peace.
                    Non-guilt is innocence.
Non-white is black.
                    Non-east
is west . . .
                    No stopping this . . .
That's why I want to spend
whatever living I have left
unlearning explanations, facts
and every other lie about
the world.
                    The only questions
worth my time will always start
and end with why.
                    I've seen
the Arab boys of Jordan
speak them with their eyes.
I sense them in my son
each time he reaches
up from sleep to read
my features with his fingertips . . .
It's not as easy as it looks.
There's more to certitude
than sound or sight.
                    There's
more than darkness to the night.

THE DRENCHING

Targeted, I know that I can die
  by lightning now.
              Or now.
                    Or now.
I slog beneath the enfilade
  of burst on burst of buckshot
  rivers, lakes, oceans, cesspools
  sunsucked to the clouds and spattered
  back.
          Puddles dance in rainfire.
Hopscotching, hurdling, wirewalking,
  I slip the deeper pools
  before I shrug it all to hell
  and splatter straight ahead
  like infantry.
                  Across the street
  a girl has shucked her shoes.
She wades duck-happy in the sluice
  of sewers.
              Her skirt shapes
  to her hips.
                Her sweater defines
  what sweaters define, but rainfully
  moreso.
            Laughing, she waves
  at gawkers in a bus.
                      I half-expect
  to hear, "Come in, the water's
  fine."
          Rainleaks start saucing
  in my shoes.

                    Taxis go aquaplaning
by before a double spume
of spray.
                    The skyroof cracks
with skyflash, mends and cracks
again.
                    Hatcheted by wind,
a weeping willow splits
and splinters by a fountain brimmed
to flood by the real thing . . .
Socks oozing, suit
dripping (but not quite dry
as advertised), I'm in my element.
Lightning can smash.
                            The bilging sky
can spill from here to Mars,
and I'll still balk at doorway-docks
and awning-harbors.
                            Rainlocked,
I'm free of how my clothes
presented me.
                    But still I'm stuck
with them, and still they drag
me down.
                    By the waters of Babylon
Boulevard, I bear them like a cross
beneath a kingdom come
of thunder.
                    A bus maneuvers
like an ark adrift with prisoners.

She of the sculpting sweater
saunters in gutterwater.
A boy in overalls wades by,
licking his strawberry cone
as if nothing's happening.

In Cairo, belly dancers,
   to be sure—one to a hotel
   like a doorman or concierge.
In the Hotel Cleopatra
   a blonder Cleopatra shakes
   with Nasser's necessary
   cellophane across her navel.
But the streets are something
   else.
         En route to Giza—
   camel manure steams
   in the gutters.
           A boy with flies
   on his lips badgers *baksheesh*
   before he hunches on his hams.
Under his sleeving gown,
   flies speckle his testicles . . .
Around the pyramids, drivers
   hawk their camels.
             "Come,
  effendi.
        Take a ride,
   and you will look like Lawrence
   of the Arabs."
           Crowned with a loop
   of rag, I pitch between
   the rocking humps toward
   the Sphinx like Caesar, Alexander,
   Bonaparte, the first and final
   Pasha, Churchill, Rommel,
   Conrad Hilton—all
   in one.

Up close, the mirror
of the Sphinx shows nothing new.
The sleeping animal with anybody's
face remains the image
of my kind.
                    In stone, it cannot
hide.
           In flesh, it shimmies
to a drum, begs bread,
reins camels for a tip,
unfurls the puny banners
of itself and then turns
poet in its own defense.

Once for the Last Bandit

THE DAY AFTER YESTERDAY

Each night the gallivanter
   that I was won't die.
Each day I cut the deck
   with him.
        He wins.
               I win.
Who are the twins called me
   who can't be young or old?
I put my question to the sun.
Before I was, it is.
After I'm not, it is.
The sixth day of God
   is when the earth's clock
   stopped.
        I am the seventh
   day and ticking, ticking.

SPARK

My pen stalls.
>> I'm rubbing
> stick on stick to spark
> a word.
>> Why not?
>>> Who knows
> what makes a poem flare
> and spurt across a page?
It's not that I'm without
> alternatives.
>>> I could walk,
> play music, read, plan
> for the lie of the future, sleep.
Instead, I choose this
> slow unraveling of me
> in what I see and all
> I see in me, this scrivening
> of oaths, this servitude, this ransom.

AZIMUTHS

My place?
                What is my place
if where I am is where
I'm not?
                Forget cartography.
I dream myself through walls,
walk Mars at will, shoot
azimuths that arrow down
the stars.
                Ferret the heart
of thieves, and there I hide.
Along the flying carpet
of a jet, I pass my face
repeated down an aisle.
                            Before
the blinkless peering of the blind,
I have no eyes.
                A town
of starving, black Pinocchios
so limply shrinking into death
can shrivel me to tears.
Without my choice, I'm cast
from role to role and back
again—no acts, scenes,
curtain.
                Playing the day's
roulette as cad, king,
clown, cock-o'-the-walk,
I am a compass dropped,
the needle dancing east,
south, west, then steadying,
steadying north to me.

BELLBEAT

The tongue of the bell must bang
   the bell's cold shell
   aloud to make the bell
   a bell.
           No otherwise exists.
What else is every iron
   peartop but an iron
   peartop if it simply cups
   its centered stamen still?
The frozen pendulum strikes
   nil.
        It plumblines
   down like double hands
   made one at half past six.
I've seen the carilloning
   tulips battened down
   in belfries.
           I've heard them
   rock and creak in rainy
   winds.
         I've felt the dangled
   nubs inch close to sound
   but never close enough
   before the muting night
   enshrines them in their brass
   monotony.
         It takes the tugging
   down and easing up
   on one lowknotted rope
   to jell the shape and sound
   of what remembers to become
   a bell.

And gong it goes,
it goes, it goes . . .
And tones go sheeping over,
after, under one
another, shuddering in high
cascades from quick to quiet.
The muffled bellbeat
in my chest rhymes every
beat of the bell with breath.
It tolls my seven circles
in the sun.
It thunders in my
wrists.
It does not rest.

LOST SWIMMER

Each poem I surprise from hiding
is a face I learn to draw
by drawing it.
                    Masterplan?
None.
          Strategy?
                        None except
whatever wits I pit
against myself to bring it
off.
          Never the face
imagined nor a face in fact,
my making is its own solution.
It tells me how it must
become, and I obey or else.
I see myself as some
lost swimmer of the night
who must discover where
he goes by going.
                        Uncertain,
dared and curious, I stall
my dive until the surface
stills its saucered ditto
of the moon.
                    Then, plunge . . .
Sleep's inland waves lock over
me.
          Ashore, the sealevel
world of pistols, porkchops,
mirrors and garbage ripens
into headlines.

But where I
plummet, horses ride on wings,
water burns, and willows
write their reasons in the wind.
The pure imagination of a dream
is mine to swim until
the baiting light betrays
me.
And I rise.
The shore
steadies where I left it.
The whole
unfloatable and failing world
goes by as given.
I swim
from maybe to the merely real
and make them one with words.
I wonder how I did
it.
I wondered how I'll do
it.
And I've done it.

VOODOO

Profession?
          Wordsmith.
                         Ambition?
Only to leave American
  no worse because I wrote it.
Failings?
                Truculence beyond
reason.
             Tell me I can't
be disappointed and believe,
and, disappointed, I'll go on
believing.
                Suggest I roam
for inspiration, and I'll say
the knife I hone in my own
room would cut no keener
in Japan, Geneva or the Hebrides.
Call poetry the voodoo of the mad,
  and I'll explain how madness
keeps me sane.
                    Better mad
than futile.
                Defenses?
                       Search
me, and you'll find no
loaded automatic hidden
in my pocket like pornography, no
shield except an aging
epidermis fuzzed with hair,
no tactic but the ruse of trust.
Results?

Who knows?
It's still
the price of love to fight
the battle for the future now
and lose.
At least I know
what I'll say no or yes to
long before I must.
Meanwhile,
I stay a breath away
from God and write down what
I just remember.
A word here . . .
A phrase there . . .
Not much
to memorize unless a consecration
comes to make them worth
remembering.
But if and where
it comes, then watch me stitch
my dreams to syllables, connive
with pens like some magician
in a frenzy, shake to hell
this seven-come-eleven world
and make what's happening my heaven.

RELICS

I'm writing ruins of myself
Don't laugh.
                    If I say poets
    are their poems, who
    says no?
                    What more is Plato
    but his Greek?
                            Forget the wax
    museum of biography.
                                Relics
    remember realer faces.
Completely incomplete, they live
    the life we let them live.
Take Thebes.
                    Imagination's
    history of history assembles
    temples in the skull.
                            Take
    Boomtown, California.
                            The doors
    of taverns document the winds.
Take me.
                    My archeology amounts
    to dots and slashes on a page.
Within the status quo
    of fire, soil, wind
    and wave, I'm salting down
    to driftwood.

             Call me my
souvenirs.
             The ink of blood
won't dry.
             What you
agree I mean, I mean.

FROM ROCK

His marble goddesses stare
   everything to dust but rock.
No pupils at their cores,
   their eyes are noons without
a sun.
       Gently they weather
in the wind that flags the sculptor's
match to my cigar.
          "Do you
believe in God?" he probes.
"Some time."
         "When, mostly?"
Benignities of stone are listening.
Their eyes hear all.
      "Outglare
us if you dare," they say.
"What shares the ages of the sun
   has no competitors.
         Creation
is our birthday."
        The sculptor
wonders, "When?"
         "Working
at what I love."
      "I, too."
Queen after queen confesses
   him the hewer, him
   the conjurer who fretted her
   from rock until she sang . . .
"When God made stones, He made
   them all at once forever,"
he resumes and coasts his palm
across a bust of flint.

"Like gems, they tell you how
  they must be cut.
                    You must
  be sparing.
                  Less is more.
You must respect the action
  of the stone."
                  Eye by eye
  the chanting goddesses agree,
  "We are the fifth and surest
  element.
              To fire, water,
  earth and air, add rock.
Add certitude.
              Add us."

Bridging forty, I've lived
   already longer than I thought.
Call it survival.
              Call
   it the chance to last
   by chance.
           This side
   of promises, the only life
   I realize is how I live
   this minute.
            I counted dimes
   while Fagan lost his knees
   and Elmore died of shrapnel
   in the eyes.
           A flowerpot
   dropped thirty-seven
   stories in New York
   on someone else's skull.
I missed the whisperjet
   that ploughed Lake Michigan.
Lazarus walks in my shoes,
   and Lazarus meets my mirrored
   eyes each time I brush
   my teeth.
           That's why I'm slow
   to trust tomorrow's men,
   men shaped to a role,
   vehicular.
          They are the self
   I shed.

Brothered to blood
that stays an ageless red,
I wage no other disciplines
than bladder, bowel, mind
and tongue.
                    Breath by death,
they root me to myself
in everyone.
                    To stay abreast
I spend the better part
of better days than I deserve
making poems in American.
That way I earn my way,
leaving epitaphs that show
and slow me as I go . . .
Wordpriest—penman
in transit—God's plagiarist.

OF RIGHTS AND ROUTES

Challenging the pure sloth
  of fog, I steer through now
  or never.
              The time is Pennsylvania.
The place is always.
                  Under
  and behind me, the mountain
  I ascend descends.
             If I
  could taxi from the peak
  and soar for stars, I'd zoom
  at sixty seconds a minute
  to somewhere more than
  Hazo in hell or heaven . . .
The wax melts.
           No longer
  Adam, not yet Christ, I fall
  into mortality.
              Fogged in, I guess
  directions.
           The towns say
  welcome.
          Deny or die
  remains the church's cry.
The state says don't make
  trouble for the state.
              Crossing
  the meanwhile world of rights
  and routes, I'm bogged in deeper
  fogs.

When darkness lightens
into clearings, I try to find
some way to have my say.
Sculptors who sledge from utter
rock the courage of their hearts
could tutor me.
                    Dante
from the horn of hell could be
my guide.
            Instead, I'm left
with me.
            The tires on the strips
are thrumming, thrumming.
                        Windshield
wipers arc from dark to dark,
the headlights drill for distance,
and the road keeps coming.

AT BAY

A car door shuts
  like a shell.
          My sleeping ears
  record the clicktight
  of grease and tumblers.
              Who's
    coming?
        Voices volley
  away, away.
            Pitchnight
  slides back like ocean
  to a beachpock, drowning
  carbeams and echoes with itself.
But doors keep closing
  in my ears.
        Voices limbo
  on and leave the night
  like shaken snow unsettled
  in a globe.
          I'm jailed with chairs
  at attention, doors awaiting
  knuckleknocks, the passive
  poise of telephones that may,
  at any second, ring.
            Under
  the stars, leaf after leaf
  in falldeath die and fall
  by hillsides into cracklesweeps.
The winds are at them.

                              Willows
change to plumes.
                    The moon
deflects one quarter of the sun
across my arm.
                    Chairs distance
the walls.
                    Walls keep winds
at bay.
            Shadows of stormy
leaves mimic the sway
of queens in grief.
                    I'm one
among so many.
                    I know
myself by what I'm not.
What nothing is, I am.

LAST TOUCH

The breadwarm sun speckles
   what I left: a pen,
   a notebook, Santayana's essays
   marked at page sixteen.
I play the peak of Pike,
   a brick on a roof, the sprung
   clock that says it's half
   past now forever.
                Words
   stall in the capped pen.
My notebook yawns for thoughts.
Page seventeen of Santayana
   sleeps to bloom in the sun
   of mine or anybody's eyes.
They wait.
         I wait.
             To live
   I must resume, make coffee,
   friends, money, amends,
   invent a poem.
          To stop
   I must be stopped.
            Summoned
   unexpectedly away, silenced
   at last touch, I'll
   cease before I'm finished.

Four
Februaries back, while suds
burst in the sink and coffee
percolated and the television flipped
and flipped, my aunt dropped
to her knees against a chair
dead.
Screening my own
stopped film of pen,
book, page and now
this poem donkeying in mid-
line, I think of that.

ALMANAC

This game of numbering the strokes
  of light must stop.
                Moses
  denied the seventh day
  of God if all he saw
  was sunburst and arithmetic.
Sun's day . . .
           As if each day
  weren't just as much
  the sun's as yesterday's
  tomorrow . . .
             I look for suns
  without a name or number.
I walk the altar of this earth
  that tombs the bones and relics
  of my kind, that floors
  the breathing cross of each
  of us until we topple.
Don't almanac the light
  for me.
          The gospel of winter
  wind is time enough.
Tulips bloom epiphanies.
A sparrow sings its own
  morning, and grass strikes
  green without a chime.

THE SUM

To date I've swallowed lakes
  of coffee, water and assorted
  liquids, eaten farms
  of lettuce, grapes, tomatoes,
  beef by the herd, hens
  by the flock, a year's haul
  of fish.
        I've smoked enough
  tobacco for a clan, outworn
  a shop of shoes, scanned
  libraries, crossed seven
  of the world's great rivers,
  traveled forty times
  around the earth without
  leaving the country, faced
  legions of students, earned
  half a million, plus or minus . . .
I'm not the sum of all
  these parts.
        One plus one
  equals nothing but now—
  and now dies in the saying.

SKYCOAST

I'd build a house with windows
   in the roof so I could see
   from underneath the plunge
   and spatter of rain, snow
   in a bluster, hail hitting . . .
Having a skycoast would
   liven me more than living
   near the sea.
              No sound.
                       No

smell.
        No villainy.
                  Air
is my element.
              It's pitch
   and pressure keep me
   as and what I am.
No one can drown in it.

IN GREEN AISLES

A dock of concrete shudders
  to a shunting locomotive
  inching freight, the blind
  but perfect coupling of caboose
  and car, the buried ganglions
  of steam.
                Hoses hiss
  in soot.
                Conductors watch
  like extras in a moviescript,
  postdated by their uniforms
  to regulated years of schedules
  and no air.
                Gauntlets of twin
  sleepers fence me in green
  aisles.
                Their stenciled names
  could be the names of scents
  or thoroughbreds—"Cherry City,"
  "Marford," "Cedar Canyon,"
  "Alshazar."
                Blind after drawn
  blind shuts me out.
It is something to snore
  through cities, to smoke a slow
  cigar in dark roomettes,
  to dream of waking in Chicago,
  Kansas City, Abilene,
  to toss with locomotion, slowly
  to raise the blind a fraction
  midway through Ohio, to see
  a cornfield dog or, all
  at once, Sandusky, prairies

obstacled with shocks, lights
in a kitchen, silos glistening
with dew, a fieldscape waging
utter quiet in the first
mass of frost, the lifted
wafer of the sun ascending
double through the pullman
windows, limning the sleek
rails forward to yesterday.

MY SEALED AQUARIUM

Seatbelted for the worst,
  I slither into traffic like a trout.
Downstream, down
    sluicing ramps, down
    capillary boulevards, down
    freeway Mississippis,
    I ogle from my sealed
    aquarium and swim with schools
    in the current.
               Fish-eyed
   in glass, I minnow sideways
   to the blink of go and stop.
I race the passing gills.
I trail the leadering fins.

THE REST OF ME

Down right, the lights of Cincinnati.
Down left, the mingled rainbows
  of Toledo, Pontiac, Detroit.
Below, Ohio's midnight
  polkadots.
              Soaring the strict
  parabola between Chicago
  and New York, I'm strapped
  in place at seven miles
  a minute.
              Wings go; I
  watch . . .
              Legs go; I follow . . .
Wheels go; I ride . . .
              Coolied
  by my feet or chaired in taxis,
  buses, trains through ploughed
  canals of snow, through halls,
  through speeding and retreating
  Illinois, I keep erect
  from neck to crotch.
              Even
  when I run, only my legs
  are busy.
              The rest of me
  is moved along unmoving
  to the anywhere I occupy so
  instantly.
              There stays there
  before my coming changes it
  to here.

Here is here
until my going names it
there again.
Gypsied, my senses
scout their five horizons.
Beyond arm's length, there's
nothing I can touch.
I'm blind
to distance and the dark.
Between
loud silence and the merest
crash, I keep my ears undeaf.
The clam of my mouth must gorge
before I relish.
And my nose?
One pinch can nix that terrier.

QUICKENINGS

Watching the turbojets approach,
  what makes me dream of divers
  lancing down to blue, their arms
  still swanned, their eyes willed
  shut beneath their winging brows
  and sleeked helmets of hair?
Around me—New Hampshire.
The mountains are having it out
  with April, staying the March
  ice in streams, basing
  like pincushions the spindles
  of a million trees without a pin
  of green.
              Balked in a skyport
coffeeshop, I'm booked to sail
the air for home.
                    But while
I wait, my blood rebukes
me, damns what bridles
it with schedulings and rouses
me to know what I can learn
by listening.
                The wind has no
o'clock.
            It summons me aboard
my plane on time ahead
of time as if I've been
aboard before.

I know
the look of mountains from above
before I see them from above.
No matter when I turn,
the world is where I was.
My future seems a film rolled
last to first, reeling
the diver in me up from blue
to risk again the risk
I've taken.
                    Nothing waits.
Old quickenings keep forging
me ahead as April forges
May from branch to branch.
The wind keeps billowing the twin
bellows of my lungs.
                         It runs
to ride me from and to
myself.
            Nowhere and any time
is where it's been
and how it is and goes.

SKYSWIM

In any skyswim, climb
   from deep to deeper.
                         Look
   straight down at birdfish,
   seaweed-and-sargasso clouds,
   thunderboulders, underwater
   moss of farms, coral
   cities and the graveyard cars
   asprawl like pieces of eight
   between the phlox of towns.
Let sharks that pass you
   keep their altitudes like baits
   suspended at fixed fathoms.
Who cares how deep you go?
The top of the blue is where
   you level off and where
   your staying makes it so.

WHERE IT WAS

An echelon of ducks veers
overswamp like some lost
squadron from the world's last
war.
     Unstuttering they go
before and after buckshot
buckles one.
     Crumpling, it
falls from a white flakburst
of feathers.
     It leaves the memory
of where it was.
     The feathers,
one by three by five,
come fallingleafing down.
The echelon ascends.
     The place
where the duck would have been
rises and soars with the flock.

IMPALED

A kite skyloops and spins
   on spiking limbs to swing
   there, crucified.
                   Too high
   for any pole to lance it
   loose, it trails its drifting
   line and stays.
                   How many
   snows will leave a skeleton
   of two crossed sticks
   impaled on branches leafing
   into April?
                   Something in me
   wants to set it free.
Something in me doesn't.

SMITHEREENS

Skull of a bull . . .
             Whitening,
  the bone turns conjurer
  to recollect the steer who mounted
  cows in utter boredom,
  hoofed through dung and butted
  in brute fury the caping
  flies.
             Gored by the horn
  of truth, I heed what hides
  in smithereens.
                     What am
  I but a smithereen myself?
Among all past and present
  images of God, I live
  complete but still a part
  of what the integer of me
  completes.
             Trillions remain
  divisible by me.
                     Raise
  me to any power possible,
  and I identify myself
  in multiples of everyone
  and anywhere.
             Fragment
  by fragment, I piece my own
  mosaic of the world.
                     Soaring
  over Lesbos, I remember all
  that's left of Sappho's oracles.
Like crumbs of rock I swiped

from the Acropolis, her talismans
unbury Greece.
                    Shepherds
flock their ewes.
                    A lover
flexes in a hug of thighs
to seed from scratch our first
mythologies.
                    What more is
matching but a match of fractions?
What afterlock of loins
shelled Venus from the sea
or posed her naked on de Milo's
pedestal?
                    Intact, her torso
breeds no mystery.
                    Only
the arms that are not there
are there for anyone's imagining,
and armlessly she beckons us.
In time and out of time
she hunts me to my last
division.
                    Is she God's virgin
or the bitch of trumps?
                                In punctual
Geneva she awakens me
while pigeons chortle back
the night, inching the morning
on until it candles
everywhere at once.
Near Evian she plays Pandora
    to the wind and harps the pinwheel

spokes of bikers into hymns . . .
In Istanbul the immemorial,
she chants a thought of Harry
dying in the States.
                    "Poems
create what prose is left
to talk about."
                    In Sariyer,
Daglarca finishes what Harry
meant.
          "Poems are letters
from our closest friends."
                              In Turkish
or American, these prophecies
deliver me.
              I hammer ashes
from my pipe and sow them
where the continents divide
Byzantium.
              The sutures of the earth
will never close, and ashes
resurrect the dragon's teeth
of fear.
          A submarine from Russia
splits the Bosphorus.
                        From home
the talk is politics and guns.
A tongue inside the facts
announces to the wind what
every poet knows.
                    The rest
is history.
              The rest is prose.

MY KINGS

My best advice?
            No advice.
If I forget myself, don't
    listen.
            If you listen, don't
    agree.
            If you agree, don't
    say so.
            Shadowing myself,
    I want no one to track me
    as I go . . .
            At twenty, I
    was God.
            At thirty, Christ
At forty, me.
            Still unreformed,
    I can't forgive real enemies.
But I'm a straight foe.
I hate fair.
            As for the past,
    I let it pass.
            What lasts lasts.
And as for questions?
            The worst
    deserve one answer; the next
    worse, two; the second best,
    three or better; and the best,
    none.
            Voids after why
    destroy me into poetry.
            Like one
    lost and humming for company,

I write to reach the audience
I am.
                    Pauses between words
say all I want to say.
So, silence by silence
    I give myself away.
                        Each
    time I think I'm not enough
    to give, I give me away
    and waken multiplied . . .
                        Why wait
    for headlines?
                    All news
    is dated yesterday.
                    Why settle
    for the once of rulers, ragers,
    rakers, roundabouters?
                        Why
    suckle on the milk of wolves?
My kings are tulips drinking
    from their roots to find a light
    through midnight to the sun.
                        I learn
    from rivers easing seaward
    at their speed and level.
                        As rocks
    wait, I wait.
                Floating
    on my back in grass, I read
    the moon and sum the posted
    stars from one to wonder.

[155]

UNDER SIEGE

Dealer of aces, shuffler
  of trumps, stretcher of hurting,
  shrinker of grins, what
  are you but the last of all
  bandits?
              Against my will
  you leave me living for death,
  dead to the living.
                  In speed,
  in what is slow or stopped,
  in every distance of the eye
  or blood, you pressure me.
You are that start that bullets
  down the universe toward me
  since the start of stars—
  invisible but destined for collision.
I am a spider dangling
  from the gutstring of myself.
One swoop can shatter me
  and all my weavings.
                  You stay.
You win.
              I fade like Scorpio
  behind the archer's constellations.
Decade by decade, all
  my muscles slacken.
                  What
  am I but a circled soldier
  under siege?
              I shall survive
  each battle but the last.

HORIZONTALS

Hello, my opposite.
                    Two
continents apart, we breathe
as strangers on this muddy moon.
Our toes are roots.
                    Our faces
flower to the sun like nodes
of diametric poles.
                    A different
dicer's toss, and I'd be
sloshing through a swamp,
sticking my buffalo to make
him plough.
            And you?
                        Could you
accept this Florida of health
food shoppes, reducing
spas, free cardiographs
and Christian Science reading
rooms?
        Or would you stroll
as alien as I?
                Before indifferent
mirrors, I face the same
barbarian.
            Refine, refine,
refine, and still he never
changes into me.
                Conditions
right, this rogue could kill,
betray, corrupt.
                But mirror,
mirror on the wall says all

it knows is what it shows.
Barabbas with fangs?
                        Don
Juan as Mister Hyde?
                        Humped
Quasimodo slobbering his jowls?
Caliban?
                Nothing but cartoons . . .
My underman can pass for me.
Grubby for the crumbs of praise,
    he never sleeps.
                        He wants
    to solo our duet.
                        He dreams
    of fires for the moon.
                        I weaken
    into him the way a ripe
    idea rots into an ism.
Which face am I?
                        The man
    who mocks the savage I refuse
    to be or the savage in the man
    who masquerades as me?
                                Back
    to health food shoppes,
    cyclo-masseurs, audiometrists,
    corsetieres, podiatrists . . .
                                Agreed,
    to coax an extra inch
    from life is hardly damnable.
But what's the use.
                        The blood
    has no horizons.

Water
freezes everywhere the same.
Clouds rain.
All men are nine
parts sea, and down to skulls
they rhyme like egg with egg.
We're split, my seesaw-twin,
by longitudes and other accidents.
On horizontals of the simply so
we stay dead even as we go.

MY ROOSEVELT COUPÉ

Coax it, clutch it, kick it
   in the gas was every dawn's
scenario.
               Then off it bucked,
   backfiring down the block to show
it minded.
               Each fender gleamed
   a different hue of blue.
Each hubcap chose
   its hill to spin freewheeling
into traffic.
               I fretted like a spouse
   through chills and overboiling,
jacked my weekly flats
   and stuffed the spavined seats
with rags.
               Leaking, the radiator
   healed with swigs of Rinso,
brake fluid and rainwater.
                     Simonized,
   the hood stuck out like a tramp
in a tux.
               All trips were dares.
Journeys were sagas.
               From Norfolk
   to New York and back,
I burned eleven quarts
   of oil, seven fuses
and the horn.
               One headlight
   dimmed with cataracts.

                                        The other
        funneled me one-eyed
        through darker darks than darkness . . .
O my Roosevelt coupé, my first,
        my Chevrolet of many scars
        and heart attacks, where are you
        now?
                        Manhandled, you'd refuse
        to budge.
                                Stickshifted
        into low, you'd enigmatically
        reverse.
                        Sold finally
        for scrap, you waited on your treads
        while I pocketed thirty
        pieces of unsilver and slunk
        away—Wild Buck Hazo
        abandoning his first and favorite
        mount, unwilling to malinger
        long enough to hear
        the bullet he could never fire.

GAUNTLETS

Whose hound?
                  He rounds the waiting
      room, nosing for groins
      before legs shut
      in his face.
                  Impatient among
      patients, I read the clock's
      twin semaphores like elevator
      arrows stopped at someone
      else's floor.
                  The hound
      plays hound.
                  He barks us
      into shock or lolls on the rug
      to lick his shifting, itching
      bag.
            A scent of glossy
      magazines domesticates the air.
RFK, unshot and winning
      Indiana, waves from a cover
      of a dead year's *Life*.
                        By the time
      I'm summoned, Kennedy's killed
      again, the moon lassoed
      and Charles DeGaulle outvoted
      to a final cross in Colombey.
                              The sex
      of the nurse is neuter: "Your
      name?"
            Who am I
      when I say I am?
                        Myself?

The man I mean to others?
Snaking between the day's
forked branches, I ransom,
skin by skin, my worst
and best.
         Shriven, I'm free
to be the selves that other
selves complete in me.
"Address?"
         Away, I'm home.
At home, I'm always leaving.
"Your X rays show no break,
  but still the ribs need
  taping; follow me, please."
We troop gauntlets of sickrooms—
  door open, door ajar, door
  shut.
         A wheelchaired sleeper
rouses to the gunning of our heels.
I see him as a trout nibbling
  the surface air until he
  slips again into his element.
The sudden lava killed
* the people of Pompeii unwarned.*
Centuries made statues of them
* underground—in beds,*
* in fields beside a lamb,*
* in armor.*
         "I'll need
to shave your chest."
                 "No soap?"
"Dry will do."

"Your turn next?"

　　　　　　　　　　With two
good reasons not to think
that's funny, she razors nude
a patch of chest and binds
it with adhesive.
　　　　　　　　　"Come back
on Saturday."
　　　　　　　　Returning through
the urban corridors of pain,
I roam Pompeii—each room
a universe, each universe
a life, each life a sphinx
of memory that flames volcanoes
in my skull.
　　　　　　　A poem stirs.
Trivia inspire me—a bandaged
ligament, a moan, the cool
vanishing of alcohol on skin.
What makes me think that poems
make a difference?
　　　　　　　　　Socrates
and Christ wrote nothing.
Under the ticking twentieth
century I watch the hound
kicked, clapped and hooted
out.
　　　　　Condemned for being
too himself, he balks like Plato's
poet at the door.

I'm back.
My welcome is a hung jury
      of ailers counting on the worst.
Unhounded now except
      by what they came to cure,
      the firing squad of seven
      pairs of eyes confronts me.
They want to know what's up,
      what took so long, who's next?

Say you are Caesar contemplating
  Cleopatra nude on one
  plumped cushion.
                    Plump girl.
Rolled from a rug.
                    Supine.
Unlike a mother's lounging
  teats, her breasts uphold
  their sprouts.
                You trace her navel's
  tiny whirlpool with your thumb
  before your fingers wedge apart
  the Niles of her knees and . . .
                              You
  are yourself again with anyone's
  conclusions.
                The slit at the split
  of the forks can humble bums
  or Caesars to the hump of studs.
Some sailor on his frogging wench
  can twin the orgy of a hun.
The kiss of bundled Eskimos
  in love remembers Romeo's
  warm lips on Juliet's.
                        Lovers
  keep hugging on their sheets.
A tart at the Bar Parisienne,
  prettied for sale but not
  for keeping, waits for her pimp
  to send her sleeping.
                        The loins
  ache to their purpose.
                          Blind.

NOW UNALIVE

No matter when he died . . .
He died for me the minute
  I was told he died.
              Before
  I knew, I learned the fallen
  alphabet of leaves starfishing
  over lawns and boulevards.
I breathed October while
  a punted football spun
  and thudded tipsy on the turf.
Informed, I saw no more
  than what he used to be.
             He stared
  straight back from saucer rims.
I saw him coffined
  in the sky.
          He would emerge
  like trick photography
  from someone else's face.
             Living,
  he aged like any man,
  located in his skin, plotted
  by absolutes of calendars
  and clocks.
          Now unalive,
  he grows from someone into
  everywhere.
           My words reach
  out to what he is
  like lassos to the seven winds.

UNDERHOOF

Her cancering grains have bred,
  are breeding . . .
                    Arcs of the scythe
  cut near, nearer, caving
  my bowels in a cold defeat.
Outdoors, the only Monday
  that can be is happening.
Important sparrows halo
  chimney after chimney.
                      Legioning
  leaves rain in the once
  of November.
                Skull-trampler,
  I wade the sweepings of the wind.
Night buries light
  as Troy layered each declining
  Troy to forge its ninth
  and final banners.
                  Slaughterings,
  eggs that will never hatch,
  uprooted onions leaven my blood.
The pelts of stallions glove
  my feet.
              Dismembered maples
  bear my bones to sleep.
Sentenced to last by bread
  alone, I plead the death
  and rising of a Jew named God.
Four horses and their horsemen
  ride me to the last trumpets.
They ride.

They ride.
                    Someone
I scarcely know has fallen
underhoof.
                    Her silences
are requiems.
                    Someone I
scarcely know?
                    What more
am I to me, to anyone?

ZEROS

Drained to its deepwater paint,
  the swimming pool's a crater
  for the stars.
             Stakeless, the pits
  for horseshoes batten under
  mulch.
        A front page
  flattens to a fence, headlining
  law and order to a cat's
  toilet.
        Stitch by stitch,
  last summer comes apart.
I'm due for mountain highways
  and a quiet carnival of leaves
  exploding out of green, each
  color glorying with difference,
  each difference making difference
  all that difference means.
               Zeros
  from now, the similar snow
  shall say the queen's in hell
  again.
        A cemetery widens
  to my lights.
        For the seven
  hundredth time I pass it
  for the first time.

                    Granite
         crosses crop the slopes.
The grass is barbered to the inch.
The candles of planted flags
    flicker on the fresher altars.
My people molder here:
      printer, poolshark, mother,
      aunt, progenitors.
                     Alive,
      they matched in nothing but
      a name, ate eggs from the same
      plate, argued, made music
      when they gathered.
                          Now, look.
These few square yards.
                          This rank
      and file peace.
                  This midnight.

YESTERBURNINGS

The siren loudens nearer
  like a widened eye.
                   Vesuvius
  erupts in suds from bursting
  jugs of beer.
               Cheese
  butters the griddle of the floor,
  and barrels of tomatosauces
  bubble to a boil in their drums.
Upstairs, the kneaded breasts
  of dough are igloos in a row
  across a rack.
              The flames
  make bread of them before
  the cuttering siren slackens
  through a floe of smoke.
Unrolled in nothing flat,
  the flattened hoses fatten
  with plugwater.
             They nosel
  like anacondas for the blaze
  and strangle it in minutes.
By the last rolled hose,
  the pizzeria's cooling back
  to business.
            I'm anyone.
I witness.
        I leave.
             I listen
  while the tongues of fire summon
  yesterburnings back.
Ashes kindle.

Groping
through second-story smoke,
an agony of hands despairs
of rescue.
                    Shingles peel
and smolder.
                    When London chars,
I see no more than pleading
fingers and a shingle toeing
up and letting go.
                    Twin
arms keep arching
over the infernos of Cologne
and Nagasaki and the age . . .
Unscorched in my shut house,
I see in white and black
a Buddhist with a shaven scalp
ignite.
                    Breaking like coal,
he topples backward in the furnace
of himself.
                    I shut him
off.
          Deadcenter on the screen,
he shrivels to a branding ember.

BURIALS

Roof by roof the bullseye
  houses crumble into shrines.
It's snowing fire.
                The city
  that was cellophane is stilt
  on scrap of char, shrivel,
soot.
           A mongrel sniffs
  his urine steaming orange
  in the snow.
              The rest is what
  the armies left: unburied
  feces and civilians, garbage,
  cartridges, a child screaming
  at ashfall.
             Teruel, Bilbao,
Oradour-sur-Glane, Safirah,
Deir Yassin . . .
               Burials, burials . . .
Neutral, I let the newsreel
  war dissolve in station
  breaks.
           From where I watch,
  this might have been a play—
  some Punch-and-Judy fracas
  curtained by commercials.
By satellite a child's scream
  synchronizes with a face in pain.
On film the scream slackens
  safely past.
            The face stays live.
The dying zeros of the eyes
  are chanting see, see, see.

THE JACKS

Booted to the knees in brass,
  I stomp through dreams.
                 My feet
  are penances.
          Snow freezes
  to my eyeskins, and my lashes
  lock.
        Under the grunts
  of guns, my son, my son
  keeps calling me.
             I stumble
  over swamps of sleep until
  my room explodes its beaches
  in my face . . .
          Midnight.
             My wife,
  my Anne, sleeps at my right.
My son kicks down his sheet
  and yawns his eyebrows to a frown.
Numb from nightmare, I hide
  behind the days I've lived,
  poems made, miles
  driven, students known.
The inventory chokes.
            Terror's
  ace still plays the king.
The spades of death stay
  shuffled in the deck.
           Facedown
  they come.
        The dealer's blind.
I draw the jacks I am.
Father.

Poet.
                    Born
        jokers, both . . .
                            They stake
        me through the poker of my days.
Against the night's full
        house, what can I
        bid?
                    I play for time,
        time, time.
                            No one can
pass.
                    Winner takes all,
        and the spades, the spades are wild.

Down on my knees and palms
  beside my son, I rediscover
  doormats, rugnaps,
  rockerbows and walljoints
  looming into stratospheres
  of ceiling.
              A telephone
  rings us apart.
              I'm plucked
  by God's hooks up
  from Scylla through an open door,
  Charybdis in a socket, and a cyclops
  lamp that glares floorlevel
  souls away from too much
  light to lesser darknesses.
What god in what machine
  shall pluck my son?
              Amid
  the Carthage of his toys, he waits
  unplucked, unpluckable.
                          I
  gulliver my way around
  his hands and leave him stalled
  before the Matterhorn of one
  of seven stairs.
              Floorbound,
  he follows, finds and binds
  my knees with tendrils of receiver
  cord.

I'm suddenly Laocoön
at bay, condemned to hear
some telephoning Trojan offer
me a more prudential life
where I can wake insured
against disaster, sickness, age
and sundry acts of Genghis
God.
    Meanwhile, I'm slipping
tentacles and watching my
confounding namesake toddle free . . .
Bloodbeats apart, he shares
with me the uninsurable air.
We breathe it into odysseys
where everyone has worlds to cross
and anything can happen.
Like some blind prophet
cursed with truth, I wish
my son his round of stumbles
to define his rise.
    Nothing
but opposites can ground him
to the lowest heights where men
go, lilliputian but redeemable.
Before or after Abraham,
what is the resurrection and the life
except a father's word
remembered in his son?

                                  What more
     is Isaac or the Lord?
                              Breath
     and breathgiver are one, and both
     are always now as long
     as flesh remembers.
                              No
     testament but that lives on.
The torch of blood is anyone's
     to carry.
                         I say so as my son's
     father, my father's son.

REPRIEVED

My son pronounces happy
  every bouncing ball and every
  bannered sail that spinnakers
  the wind.
            The word just fits,
  and all the jails of grammar
  spring their locks.
            Forgive
  my eastering.
            The poet
  in a child dies so young.
Tomorrow he may rhyme with rank
  on rank of pawns in jackboots . . .
Leaders with overviews and no
  vision may march him numbered
  to the dogs of Mars.
            The totem
  legions of the just shall wait
  with hindsight slings to stone him
  if he falls.
            Today he walks
  reprieved.
            Blinking at dawn,
  he feels next summer waken
  in his heart.
            Not when but why
  is what he asks the wind
  and me . . .
            Cordons in my chest
  close in, close tight.
            The world
  is what it was.

It will be
what it is.
What can
I will my son that adds
one plus to presences?
Accepting
certainties, we're free.
Refusing
or confusing them, we stay
their slave.
Palm in palm,
we go from what we knew
to what we know.
I
pull him after me.
He tugs
me to the rear.
Backing
our way ahead, we are
the future that was always here.

OF RUBBLE

Encircled by an alphabet
  of rubble, he prepares.
                His eyes
  are carnivals, and all the lettered
  blocks are bricks for him
  to mason into dreams.
              Squatting,
  he lures the architect I was
  at two-years-old beside
  him on the rug.
          Cube
  by careful cube, we reconstruct
  the wall of China, Babel
  and the pyramids.
             Teetering
  the final block in place
  is all the go we need
  to dice our London bridges
  down.
        Jericho, Jericho!
Each peewee avalanche
  unmasks the same unmaking
  maker in our blood.
            I build
  alliances with God, warriors,
  poets, sculptors chipping
  statues out of rock and back
  to rock, blackjack dealers
  shuffling cards to previous
  confusions in a deck to play
  old hands anew.

The blocks
  spell back each sound I think.
The letters on their faces say
    that Dante storied them
    to God, that all of Shakespeare
    hides in them, that Webster
    mustered them on pages instantly
    outdated, always incomplete.
My son keeps building up
  and smashing down.
                    Nothing
    shapes up alike, but what
    comes down concocts identical
    salads.
            Complete, unfinished
    as the world . . .
                    Each block
  plus twenty-five compose
  the only anagram we have.
It's what our breaking
  makes of it.
                History
  dreams by for scattered men
  to shatter into names and silences
  just once again and again.

A SECOND DARK

I am my son listening
  to me, drinking the rhymes
  my lips shall never unremember,
  watching the ceiling dance
  with dreams.
                    The moon stays where
  I name it.
             My kite sleeps
  in a tree as surely as my blue
  pajamas end in socks.
I hear me telling me
  how whales fly through
  the sea, how sparrows swim
  the wind, and why the sun
  burns down.
                Never so nimble
  as Jack nor simple as Simon
  nor quick as Cinderella's prince,
  I let my stories ramble me
  from dark to dark.
               We reach
  the dark of separate sleep
  and then a second dark where
  I become my son, myself,
  my father all at once . . .
                 Softly,
  my pillow mothers me
  almost asleep, almost . . .
It's time again.

My son
tosses through his own tonight.
I grow into the forty years,
eight months and twenty
days of me.
Who drifted
islands of oystercrackers
soddenly in gumbo?
Who lighted
epitaphs in transit and bent
the bending candleflames
to silence with a single breath?
The day's last coffee
cools in my cup while I
suck pipesmoke.
Mouths
on television reveille the dying
living room with taps.
I sip, puff, doze.
Dreams of the world bleed by.

THE ODDS

Relieved for coffee, I leave
  the field in doubt.
             Seahorse
  knights oppose their darker
  brothers; bishops, bishops,
  rooks, rooks.
           Kingly
  queens and queenly kings see
  pawns deploy like snails
  in a planned panic.
             I savor
  coffee and the wars of Caesar,
  Wellington's pluck, the look
  of players brooding strategy,
  the odds, the laurels and the luck
  or doom of being here . . . or here.
Safe where he stands, dead
  if he moves, the king stands.
Seahorses glare.
          Bishops
  spire.
       One rook survives
  the strafing justice of the queen.
Pawns topple at the stroke
  of dawn in Egypt, noon
  in Singapore and dusk on Truk.
Clocking the board, time
  present cancels every
  shadow but the tense of tactics.

The blind god of gambles
    claps for quicker finishes
    and higher stakes until
    my eyeballs turn like turrets,
    my coffee drains to canteen
    vinegar, my fingers march
    a cadence on my knee.
                            Moves
    and countermoves wake musters
    in my skull.
                        Slain pieces
    rise with names and faces
    I remember, while those I pick
    to die and lie at attention
    are one by one by one
    and all at once my son.

COUNTERTHINK

Baited by February spring,
   the tulips gamble a green
   inch for the fox of March.
My boy, my green, together
   on a seesaw swing, we mime
   a pendulum that sways me
   puzzled into fear.
                See
   where the strong have led us.
Each night I wrap the bones
   of sirloins in the day's bad
   news.
           The chaff and wheat
   connive, survive.
              Today,
   my son, I see all men
   as Alamos arrayed alone
   against the worst.
               You
   and the tulips prove me wrong.
Laughing the neutral winds
   aside, you let what's happening
   happen.
           I'm cornered in my skin.
I think.
      I counterthink.

                              Retreating
        into self-defense, I save
        the man I've learned to be.
Resisting, I become my enemies.
I must grow back to why
        you know and how you see.
Against the worst there's no
        defense.
                    We swing.
                              You grow.
The tulips plummet to the sun
        and take their chances.
                              So . . .

THE DARKER NOON

We sail asleep from midnight
  to a beach named dawn.
You stir.
      I wake.
             My only
  stars are latitudes.
             Tomorrow
  is a shore we may not reach,
  so let it wait.
          Raccoons
  are floating in their hollow
  oak cocoons.
          A milkman
  boats his bottles.
           The last
  buses trundle to their docks
  across the tire-stenciled snow.
Marking the darker noon
  of the clock, the dual arrows
  fuse into a mast that tolls
    through silence to the first birds.
The seabell of a siren wakens
  you.
      My wife.
            My mate.
Let all the klaxons clang.
These temporary sheets
  are jetsam to the moon.

How love
makes one what life keeps two
is where we are and when.
No ports.
No bos'ns but ourselves.
No echo but the wake we make
to show we buccaneered that sea.

X

Behind the closed hatches
of my eyelids, you're taking
place.
　　　Your eyes are whorls
that spin the twins of me
through day, through night.
　　　　　　　　Your
eyebrows vee like wings.
Countable, your lashes mesh
and separate . . .
　　　　　　Apart by half
a block, you'd face me
faceless—someone in a dress
whose walk I'd almost place.
Farther by mountains, you'd
stand unseeable as someone
on a star . . .
　　　　　My eyeballs swim
behind their shutters.
　　　　　　　Over distances,
the clocks of absence tell
no time at all.
　　　　　I count
our nights apart like canceled
dates across a calendar—
Monday, Tuesday, Wednesday—
X . . . X . . . X.

THREE MADE ONE

The roof reverberates with trills
and paradiddles of the rain.
                           Shelled
in the shelling car, we are three
made one against the weather.
My son wipes portholes
on the window fog and looks
for submarines.
                    Watercolors
of Ohio cross the rainshield:
cows in a phalanx, tails
to the wind, heads huddled,
pelts draining.
                    From nowhere
soars a rainbow.
                    The grass
bristles and glistens to the sun's
revenge.
                    The elms shake out
their leaves.
                    A cow dries
brighter than a toweled calf.
But the rainbow . . .
                    My bride
glows in blue silver.
Russet defines my son.
                    Tomorrow
I'll remember this as I remember
ship shapes of French fries,
coffee in Egypt, Caracas
from a cablecar . . .

                              Memory's bad
          checks buy nothing back.
Ahead is where the rainbow
          shines.
                    I tell my boy we're
          heading underneath the arch
          of all that color.
                              Even when
          it fades, I tell him that.

WHAT MATTERS LAST

The journey liquidates its plan
  and planners.
                    Architecture
  scraps its overlays.
                        The child
  born is not the child
  wombed in the imagining.
                          Before
  the headlong buck of fact,
  anticipation buckles.
                        I must
  remind myself to unexpect
  what matters last until
  it happens.
                These lines shall be
  my aide-mémoire.
                    They have exceeded
  what they started out to be,
  but what I meant, they are.

Index of Titles and First Lines

Index of Titles and First Lines

Pitt Poetry Series

James Den Boer, *Learning the Way*
(1967 U.S. Award of the International Poetry Forum)
James Den Boer, *Trying to Come Apart*
Jon Anderson, *Looking for Jonathan*
Jon Anderson, *Death & Friends*
John Engels, *The Homer Mitchell Place*
Samuel Hazo, *Blood Rights*
Samuel Hazo, *Once for the Last Bandit*
David P. Young, *Sweating Out the Winter*
(1968 U.S. Award of the International Poetry Forum)
Fazıl Hüsnü Dağlarca, *Selected Poems*
(Turkish Award of the International Poetry Forum)
Jack Anderson, *The Invention of New Jersey*
Gary Gildner, *First Practice*
Gary Gildner, *Digging for Indians*
David Steingass, *Body Compass*
Shirley Kaufman, *The Floor Keeps Turning*
(1969 U.S. Award of the International Poetry Forum)
Michael S. Harper, *Dear John, Dear Coltrane*
Ed Roberson, *When Thy King Is A Boy*
Gerald W. Barrax, *Another Kind of Rain*
Abbie Huston Evans, *Collected Poems*
Richard Shelton, *The Tattooed Desert*
(1970 U.S. Award of the International Poetry Forum)
Adonis, *The Blood of Adonis*
(Syria-Lebanon Award of the International Poetry Forum)
Norman Dubie, *Alehouse Sonnets*
Larry Levis, *Wrecking Crew*
(1971 U.S. Award of the International Poetry Forum)
Tomas Tranströmer, *Windows & Stones: Selected Poems*
(Swedish Award of the International Poetry Forum)

The poems in this volume are set in the Linotype version
of Palatino, a type face designed by Hermann Zapf and
aptly named for the Italian scribe. The decorative letters
on the title page and binding are from a set of illuminated
initials presented to Cardinal Sforza in 1490.

The book was printed from the type of Warren's Olde
Style antique wove paper by Heritage Printers, Inc. The
design is by Gary Gore.